The **India Series** introduces the rich and vibrant experience that is India through a documentation of its myriad aspects — from art to architecture, history, destinations, people and the environment.

Authoritative, lavishly illustrated and written in an accessible and lively style, each book focuses on a unique aspect of India, revealing an exciting new world and providing a stepping-stone to future discovery.

The publisher gratefully acknowledges the B Arunkumar Group of Companies
and The Gem and Jewellery Export Promotion Council for their support

GREAT DIAMONDS OF INDIA

GREAT DIAMONDS OF INDIA

MONISHA BHARADWAJ

INDIA BOOK HOUSE PVT LTD

CONTENTS

Introduction

Diamonds are nature's most precious creation. These fruits of the deep earth have been prized for centuries for their rarity and remarkable beauty, enduring as symbols of love, desire and romance. Before a diamond is set in an ornament, it is likely to be billions of years old. Any effort at dating it is fraught with uncertainty as only trace elements trapped within its prismatic depths can indicate its moment of origin. While most diamonds have been found to be between 50 million and 3.5 billion years old, it is almost certain that some are even older as the special circumstances required for their creation existed only when the earth's crust was in the process of cooling.

A diamond is formed in precise but precarious conditions. Though the hardest of all gemstones, it is the simplest in composition. Made of common carbon, a substance that is plentiful and inexpensive, and is used every day as graphite in lead pencils, the diamond is among the earth's most valuable treasures. These gems crystallise at various depths beneath the earth's surface. When pressures exceeding forty kilobars and temperatures over a thousand degrees centigrade act on carbon, it crystallises into a diamond. The force of volcanoes thrusts molten rock containing diamonds upwards through pipe-like channels to the earth's crust. If this rock does not arrive in the six hundred metres of the earth's upper crust, man will never discover the diamonds it contains. Even after this, their journey is a perilous one. If these stones cool slowly as they rise, they become graphite, and if they come in contact with oxygen while they are still hot, they vapourise into carbon dioxide. If they survive this fragile birth, diamonds will last forever.

This book is a collection of facts, mysteries, stories and myths about diamonds that have a deep and long-standing connection with India. Most of the world's famous diamonds were found in India and many of those discovered elsewhere made their way into the coffers of the richest people in the country. Even after the historic plunder of the Mughal Empire in 1739, by the Persian ruler Nadir Shah, India continued to be known as the treasury of the world and her celebrated royals as well as wealthy industrialists went to astonishing lengths to acquire and keep these diamonds. The stories of these gems recreate the drama that accompanied their passage from one owner to the next, across continents and over great expanses of time. Leaving good luck or misfortune in their wake, today these stones are unequivocally linked with the fables which travelled with them.

It is perhaps true to say that many of the great diamonds of the world, some of which are now found among the collections of the crown jewels of France, Iran, Russia and England, have an association with India. Even though they lead quieter lives now, the past few centuries have been witness to their panoramic histories and adventurous escapades, which eclipse the rather tame auctions and private sales of today.

FABLED INDIAN DIAMONDS

India, is the most agreeable abode on earth,
and the most pleasant quarter of the world.
Its dust is purer than air,
and its air purer than purity itself:
its delightful plains resemble
the garden of Paradise,
and the particles of its earth are
like rubies and corals.

TAZJIYATU-L AMSAR

KOH-I-NOOR

WORTH HALF THE DAILY EXPENSE OF THE WHOLE WORLD

Weight: 105.60 CARATS
Cut/Shape: BRILLIANT/OVAL
Size: LENGTH 31.90 MM, WIDTH 36.00 MM, DEPTH 13.04 MM
Colour: COLOURLESS
Location: TOWER OF LONDON

"Take five strong men. Let the first throw a stone northward, the second eastward, the third southward, the fourth westward, and the fifth upward, into the air. Fill all the space thus outlined with gold and you will still not have achieved the value of the Mountain of Light." – Shah Shuja to Ranjit Singh when asked about the price of the Koh-i-Noor.

Queen Victoria was fifty-six when she became the empress of India in 1877. Though she never actually travelled to India, she learnt Hindi, entertained maharajas at her cream-and-butterscotch Buckingham Palace and forbade her subjects to refer to them as 'black men'. She appointed an Indian private secretary, Abdul Karim, who wore a plum-and-gold turban, cooked delicate Indian meals in the palace kitchen, and read her papers relating to India. The queen was enchanted with everything she heard about the country, but in spite of her apparent magnanimity towards her faraway colony, she was not averse to enjoying the fruits of imperial conquest.

In 1850, the East India Company presented the celebrated Koh-i-Noor to Queen Victoria along with its owner, a boy with beautiful liquid eyes, the twelve-year-old Maharaja Duleep Singh of Punjab. Duleep Singh was taught English, made a Christian, and gently led into an extravagant lifestyle. Today, the famous diamond can be seen at the Tower of London, set in the Maltese Cross at the front of the crown made in 1937 for Queen Elizabeth, the Queen Mother.

Discovered in the mines of Golconda, the Koh-i-Noor was first reported in 1304 in the ownership of Mahlak Deo, the Raja of Malwa. The next reference to it can be found

PLAYER'S CIGARETTES

VICTORIA

The Koh-i-Noor was presented to Queen Victoria by the East India Company "with humble duty" in 1850.

Babur, the founder of the Mughal dynasty, is one of the earliest recorded owners of the Koh-i-Noor.

Nadir Shah, seated on the right, is said to have exclaimed 'Koh-i-Noor', which means Mountain of Light, upon seeing the magnificent diamond that he seized from Mohammed Shah, left, in 1739.

in the *Babur Nama*, the memoirs of the Mughal emperor Babur. According to these records, Raja Bikramajit of Gwalior sent all his jewels to the fort of Agra for safe keeping during the Battle of Panipat in 1526. However, Babur succeeded in invading the fort and acquired a diamond weighing 186 (old) carats, presumably given to him as a *peshkash* or tribute. Thereafter, the stunning gem came to be known as Babur's Diamond.

Even at that time it was considered so precious that its value was compared to half the daily expense of the whole world. In later records, such as the *Akbar Nama* (a treatise on statecraft during the rule of Emperor Akbar), historians always made references to the gem's worth in incredible terms and stated it to be beyond all valuation.

There exists an alternative account of how the Koh-i-Noor came to be in the Mughal treasury. Mir Jumla, a reputed diamond dealer from Persia who was employed by the ruler of Golconda, Abdullah Qutb Shah, became entangled in an amorous dalliance with Abdullah's mother. To prevent a scandal, he was sent away to oversee the province of Carnatic where the famous diamond mines of Golconda were located. This is where Mir Jumla's fortunes took a turn for the better and he acquired the Koh-i-Noor, the most celebrated diamond of all. Around 1656, he visited the court of Shah Jahan and presented the beautiful gem to the Mughal emperor.

Babur's Diamond, as it was first called, or the Koh-i-Noor, as later researchers have affirmed it to be, passed on to subsequent rulers over the next two centuries till it was inherited by Mohammed Shah, the debauched Mughal emperor. At this time, while the great Mughal dynasty was on the wane, a new star was rising in the firmament of Persia. Nadir Shah had become a powerful force and was rapidly stretching the boundaries of his domain. The weakened throne of Delhi was a tempting prize, and after the historic battle at Karnal in 1738, Nadir Shah stormed into the Mughal capital, potent and victorious. By 1739, he conquered Delhi, made Mohammed Shah his prisoner, and seized the vast collection of crown jewels. Eager to possess the Koh-i-Noor, he earnestly searched case after filigreed case of the looted treasure, but the diamond was nowhere to be found. Many frustrated days later, a harem woman secretly informed him that the emperor always wore it in the pleated folds of his turban. On hearing this, Nadir Shah devised an elaborate plan by which he could obtain the bewitching gem. He invited Mohammed Shah to a feast, and between luscious courses, proposed an exchange of turbans in a ceremony

of friendship and brotherhood. Mohammed Shah was rendered speechless, but, unable to refuse this courtesy, he gracefully handed over his turban. Later, on seeing the gem, Nadir Shah is said to have exclaimed, 'Koh-i-Noor' (Mountain of Light), and that is how the most famous diamond in the world acquired its name.

The historic diamond, coveted by everyone who saw it, went to Persia as the proud possession of Nadir Shah. In 1747, he was murdered in his sleep by his people. The next ruler to ascend Persia's throne was Shah Rukh Mirza, Nadir Shah's fourteen-year-old grandson who inherited his grandfather's treasured diamond. The young king's rule was fraught with tension and on several occasions his adversaries tried to usurp the throne from him. Among his loyal supporters was Ahmad Abdali, an Afghan who had been one of Nadir Shah's bravest generals and went on to rule his country, Afghanistan. Indebted to Abdali for his assistance during hard times, Shah Rukh presented the Koh-i-Noor to him as a token of his gratitude.

Abdali carried the stone to Afghanistan as part of his wealth. When he died, his son Timur became the ruler who on his demise left twenty-three sons to compete for the throne. After several years of bloody squabbling, the eldest son Zaman Shah and his brother Shah Shuja escaped to Lahore and sought refuge with the Sikh ruler, Maharaja Ranjit Singh, known as the

Maharaja Ranjit Singh (facing page), *the 'Lion of Punjab', delighted in his ownership of the Koh-i-Noor. Ranjit Singh's jewels* (above) *as drawn by Emily Eden after the maharaja showed them to her in Lahore.*

'Lion of Punjab'. Shah Shuja had managed to conceal the Koh-i-Noor in his belongings before leaving his country. Ranjit Singh, aware of this delightful piece of information, tried every possible means of coercion to divest him of it, one of which was to ask for the stone as a payment for the protection that Ranjit Singh was offering to him and his family. Shah Shuja was reluctant to part with it, but Ranjit Singh persisted and in 1813, he managed to extort the fabulous gem from him. Ranjit Singh wore it with great pleasure, mounted in an armlet between two smaller diamonds.

Maharaja Duleep Singh was a mere child when the Koh-i-Noor was confiscated from him by the British.

After Ranjit Singh, a succession of weak rulers reigned over Punjab and in 1843, Duleep Singh, then still a minor, became the new maharaja. In 1849, after two Sikh wars, the British annexed Punjab and skilfully assimilated it into their empire. The unsuspecting child-ruler in silk and brocade was brought by his advisors to sign the Treaty of Lahore, which was put before him by Lord Dalhousie, the British governor-general. The treaty included a clause which stated that the Koh-i-Noor must be handed over to the queen of England.

On its journey from Lahore to London, the Koh-i-Noor survived several near-mishaps. When in the custody of John Lawrence, an official of the Punjab government, it once lay forgotten in the pocket of his waistcoat that

The Koh-i-Noor, set between two smaller diamonds, was worn by Maharaja Ranjit Singh in an armlet, which now contains a large crystal model of the diamond.

he had tossed on a chair after a day of hard work. When asked for the gem much later, he realised with a jolt what had happened and hastened to his room to fetch it. Panic-stricken at the prospect of losing the diamond, he called for his bearer and asked him if he had seen a little box in his waistcoat pocket. The servant produced the box. With a growing sense of trepidation, Lawrence opened it, and greatly relieved, lifted out the valuable gem. The servant who had been observing him all along, remarked dryly, "There is nothing here, Sahib, but a bit of glass."

But, usually the diamond drew a more ardent response. Everyone who saw the gem was struck by its beauty, and Lord Dalhousie who brought it from Lahore to Bombay, wrote about the Koh-i-Noor in 1850, "I... never was so happy in all my life as when I got it into the Treasury at Bombay. It was sewn and double sewn into a belt secured round my waist, one end of the belt fastened to a chain round my neck. It never left me day or night...." The Koh-i-Noor finally sailed from Bombay on April 6, 1850 on the HMS *Medea* in the safe custody of Captain Ramsay.

The British public was invited to see the famous Koh-i-Noor, which held pride of place at the Great Exhibition of 1851 at the Crystal Palace in Hyde Park, London.

On July 3, 1850, it was presented to Queen Victoria at Buckingham Palace. The queen and her consort, Prince Albert, had been eagerly awaiting this marvellous acquisition but were somewhat disappointed by its lack of fire. In consultation with Garrard, the crown jewellers, the queen ordered the Koh-i-Noor to be recut. This formidable task was assigned to Voorzanger – the foremost cutter of the reputed Dutch firm Coster – who travelled to London to commence his work. The process took thirty-eight days and cost £8,000. The result was an oval brilliant weighing 108.93 carats, about a 43 per cent reduction of the

Queen Alexandra wearing a breathtaking collection of jewellery. The Koh-i-Noor can be seen in her Imperial Crown.

original weight. Unfortunately, the recutting, which caused a colossal loss of weight, failed to greatly enhance the brilliance of the stone.

The queen enjoyed her new gift, albeit an obligatory one. However, she probably felt uneasy about its acquisition as on one occasion she is said to have enquired from Lady Login, Duleep Singh's guardian, if he resented the diamond's confiscation. On April 1, 1853, the Koh-i-Noor was finally entrusted to Garrard for setting. It was mounted in a radiant tiara that contained 2,000 diamonds and cost £60,000. The gem was worn by Queen Victoria for five years, after which it was reset in a circlet. In 1902, it was set again, in the Imperial Crown, for her daughter-in-law Queen Alexandra,

THE TOWER OF LONDON

on the occasion of her coronation, and again in 1911 for Queen Mary's coronation in an ornament called the Queen Mary's Crown.

In 1937, the diamond was the premier jewel in the coronation crown made for Queen Elizabeth, the present Queen Mother, which she still enjoys wearing on state occasions. Believed to be unlucky for male rulers, the Koh-i-Noor has only adorned queens since its arrival in England.

It is only natural that a diamond as valuable and beautiful as the Koh-i-Noor, whose weight is now ascertained to be 105.60 carats, should invite controversy regarding its true ownership. Soon after India gained independence in 1947, its government asked for the diamond to be returned, but in vain. They made another unsuccessful attempt in 1953, at the time of the coronation of Queen Elizabeth II. In 1976, the prime minister of Pakistan, Zulfikar Ali Bhutto, wrote a letter to the British prime minister, James Callaghan, requesting the return of the gem. Though this was refused, Britain assured Bhutto that the diamond would not be given to any other country as its history was unclear and only Britain had a claim to it, considering that the Koh-i-Noor had been received as a gift by the queen. Even today, Britain endorses its ownership of the diamond, inviting the public to view it at the Jewel House in the Tower of London, where it is displayed as a symbol of British national heritage.

The Koh-i-Noor, set in the coronation crown (facing page) *of Her Majesty, Queen Elizabeth, the Queen Mother, is on permanent display at the Tower of London* (above).

GREAT MUGHAL
THE LOST TREASURE

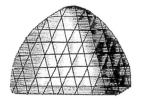

"I have seene one with the great 'Mogor' as bigge as a Hen's egge and of that very forme. ..." – H de Montfart, traveller to India, 1608, referring to the Great Mughal diamond. This drawing of the Great Mughal was made by the French gem merchant, Jean-Baptiste Tavernier.

Weight: 280 CARATS
Cut/Shape: MUGHAL HIGH ROSE/HALF OF AN EGG
Owner/Location: UNKNOWN

India was a land resplendent with lustrous gold and silver, glittering gems, shimmering silks, exotic spices and beautiful artefacts. Its rich soil yielded fabulous diamonds, whose beauty and size lured covetous European treasure hunters to its shores in the 15th century. Of all the diamonds found here, the largest to be recorded to date is the Great Mughal. As in the case of all historic gems, this diamond's past is ambiguous.

The Great Mughal was discovered in the Kollur mine in Golconda in 1650, during the reign of the Mughal emperor Shah Jahan. However, it is his son and heir Aurangzeb who is irrevocably linked with this amazing stone. Jean-Baptiste Tavernier, the French jeweller and gem merchant, left priceless records of his travels in the East in the 17th century. In *Travels in India* he claimed to have seen the Great Mughal in Aurangzeb's treasury. Tavernier wrote of a diamond that once weighed 787.50 carats but which was later shoddily cut down to 280 carats by a Venetian lapidary by the name of Hortensio Borgio, in residence at Aurangzeb's court. The emperor found Borgio's work unacceptable and fined him.

In the light of later analysis, there are certain issues that remain unaddressed in Tavernier's account. It is well known that in the East size was preferred to brilliance, so how was it that Borgio, whose work must have taken a year or more, was allowed to continue unmonitored till he had ground the gigantic stone down to a mere 280 carats? Such a historic blunder would surely have been mentioned somewhere in the records kept by Aurangzeb's courtiers, but there is no such reference. How, then, did this unfortunate incident go unwritten in the Mughal emperor's memoirs? According to the Indian historian N B Sen, local Indian cutters during that time were considered more skilful and experienced than their Western

A miniature painting depicting Prince Khurram, later to be crowned Emperor Shah Jahan, presenting a tray of jewels and other rare gifts to his father, the Mughal emperor Jahangir.

counterparts, so it seems unlikely that Aurangzeb would have assigned the task of cutting such a valuable and unique diamond to Borgio.

Notwithstanding Tavernier's detailed report, the question remains as to what mishap could have befallen the gem for it to drop out of existence so mysteriously. Gemmologists the world over have compared the Great Mughal with the Darya-i-Noor, the Koh-i-Noor and the Orlov, in the hope of finding a link. Pale pink in colour, the Darya-i-Noor is intrinsically different from the Great Mughal, which has never been described as pink. The Koh-i-Noor has a provenance dating back to the 14th century, much before the Great Mughal was found in Golconda, hence they cannot be the same diamond.

It is clear that there are similarities between Tavernier's drawing of the Great Mughal and photographs of the Orlov. The most obvious one is the shape – both diamonds have been likened to the half of an egg, which is in itself a unique distinction.

The 17th-century French jeweller, Jean-Baptiste Tavernier, left invaluable records of his travels in India.

Moreover, the Orlov has a slight indentation, which may be the "slight crack and a little flaw" mentioned by Tavernier in his description of the Great Mughal. Another peculiar fact which links the two diamonds is that the history of the Great Mughal has no particular ending, whereas the origin of the Orlov is not known.

In spite of these similarities between the Great Mughal and the Orlov, there exists a discrepancy in relation to their weight. After Borgio's folly, the Great Mughal was reduced to a mere 280 carats from the originally impressive 787.50 carats, whereas the Orlov's weight is universally recorded as 189.62 carats. However, this disparity can be explained by the fact that gemmologists are almost certain that Tavernier made a mistake in recording the weight of the Great Mughal during his visit to Aurangzeb's court.

In a study of the Russian Crown Jewels, Alexander E Fersman, the well-known Russian authority on gems, authenticated the beautiful Orlov to be none other than the Great Mughal which had so impressed Tavernier. Fersman based his conclusion on the premise that there cannot be many diamonds of such great weight that are, at the same time, so similar in appearance and composition. Often when gemmologists juxtapose the lattice of history and form of two diamonds, it emerges that the fit is perfect and that the two gems are indeed one and the same. This seems to be true in the case of the Great Mughal, which is now acclaimed as the Orlov diamond that holds a position of great distinction in the display of the Russian Diamond Fund in Moscow.

Mughal-cut diamonds remained fashionable in India right up to the time of independence in 1947.

ORLOV

"His eyes are the Sun, with the power to see, and His eyelids are both day and night."
– A description of Lord Vishnu in the Bhagvat Purana.

Weight: 189.62 CARATS
Cut/Shape: MUGHAL HIGH ROSE/IRREGULAR OVAL
Size: LENGTH 47.60 MM, WIDTH 34.92 MM, DEPTH 31.75 MM
Colour: BLUISH GREEN TINT
Location: KREMLIN, MOSCOW

The Orlov, one of the most important gemstones in the great collection of jewels of the Russian Diamond Fund, is displayed in the Kremlin in Moscow. Likened to the half of a pigeon's egg, this clear Indian diamond is mounted at the top of the Imperial Sceptre that was made for the Russian empress Catherine the Great. Estimated to have 180 facets, the gem is slightly indented on one side.

The Orlov's origins are vague, though it is presumed to have come from Golconda. An early account reveals that it was set as one of the eyes of a reclining idol of Ranganatha (another name for the Hindu god Vishnu), in the temple of Srirangam near Tiruchchirappalli in south India. According to this story, a French grenadier working in Pondicherry deserted his army and moved near Srirangam. When he heard about the remarkably precious eyes of the idol, he schemed to steal them, but it was to take him several years of plotting as only Hindus were allowed into the inner recesses of the temple. Slowly but surely, he won the trust of the Brahmin priests, first by converting to Hinduism and then by becoming an ostensible devotee of Ranganatha. This gained him access to the inner sanctum and the idol.

One monsoon night, as thunder and lightning played an eerie duet, the Frenchman stealthily crept into the temple with only flashes of lightning to guide his steps. As he gouged out one diamond eye, he felt an inexplicable fear wash over him and leaving the other eye behind, he fled for his life to Madras. Here, he sold the diamond for £2,000 to an English sea captain who carried it to London. After passing through several hands, it finally came into the possession of Khojeh Raphael, an Armenian Jew who had travelled from Persia to India, then to London and eventually to Russia. But if this account is reliable, what became of Ranganatha's other diamond eye?

Another story says that the Orlov first belonged to the Mughal emperors and was carried off by Nadir Shah of Persia after he plundered Delhi in 1739. Years later, soon after his murder in 1747, an Afghan soldier

appeared in Bassorah (about 12.8 km from the present city of Basra), north
of the Persian Gulf, with a bag of jewels and a beautiful large diamond.
The soldier, wanting to dispose of his booty, met with Grigori Safras,
an Armenian merchant who lived there with his two brothers. Safras said
that he needed time to collect enough money to buy the tantalising
diamond. Suspicious of the merchant's delaying tactics and fearing foul play,
the Afghan left the city furtively. He travelled to Baghdad, where he sold
the diamond to a Jewish trader. Not long after, Safras and his brothers
caught up with him, and extracting the name and whereabouts of the buyer,
left, determined to acquire the gem this time. However, the Jewish man
refused to part with his treasure and Safras, overcome by avarice, murdered
him. After killing the trader, he disposed of the Afghan as well for fear that
he would expose the crime.

When the question of the division of the loot arose, none of the
brothers was willing to give up the diamond. Naturally, it could not be split
into three and so the wicked Safras killed his two brothers. After this
unmitigated rampage of violence, he moved to Amsterdam to start life
afresh. Announcing himself as a dealer of jewels, he showed the diamond to
several members of the
European royalty.
Among these was
Catherine the Great,
the empress of Russia
from 1762 to 1796,
who invited him to
St Petersburg. Safras
quoted his price but
the court jeweller,
I L Lazarev, hatched
a plan to prise the
diamond away from
him through devious
means. Lazarev gently
persuaded Safras to live
a life beyond his means
in the hope that,
steeped in debt, he

*Catherine the Great, Empress
of Russia, had the Orlov set in
the Imperial Sceptre.*

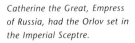

Grigori Grigorievich Orlov, a Russian nobleman and paramour of Catherine the Great, after whom the diamond was named.

would be forced to sell the diamond to the empress at the price she wanted. Though his life of excess led him to owe a great deal of money to many people, Safras refused to part with his precious stone. Instead, he garnered enough funds to pay off his debtors and left St Petersburg, determined never to return.

In yet another account, it is said that the Orlov was acquired by Count Grigori Grigorievich Orlov, a Russian nobleman and the paramour of the Grand Duchess Catherine, consort of Grand Duke Peter. When Grand Duke Peter became Tsar of Russia, Orlov and his younger brother led an uprising against him. The tsar was murdered and Catherine ascended the throne. She then wished to marry Orlov, but her political advisors dissuaded her. As time went by, Orlov fell out of favour and she began taking other lovers. Heartbroken and dejected, he left for Amsterdam, where on hearing about Safras' beautiful gem, resolved to buy it for his lost love. He presented the diamond to Catherine as proof of his love and she had it set at the top of the Imperial Sceptre, designed for her by the famous jeweller, Troitnoki. However, Orlov was never restored as Catherine's favourite. He later became demented and died a miserable death in Russia.

The contradiction to this story lies in a document allegedly signed by both Orlov and Lazarev, stating that Orlov had just been a middleman between Catherine and the seller of the diamond. She had assigned Orlov this task and had rewarded him amply by naming the diamond after him.

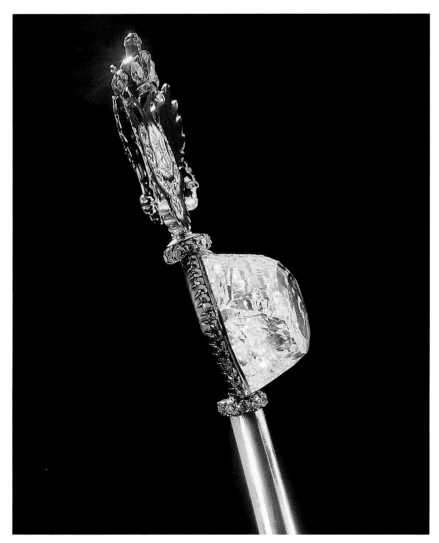

The Imperial Sceptre, in which the Orlov is set, was designed by the famous jeweller Troitnoki.

Through all these centuries, the temple of Srirangam has endured, and the serenely sleeping Ranganatha has remained oblivious to the fables of intrigue and lust that surround his missing jewelled eyes. While millions of devotees visit the shrine each year to venerate Ranganatha, the Orlov, his legendary eye, holds pride of place in the public display of the crown jewels of Russia, also attracting millions of fascinated visitors every year.

Pigot

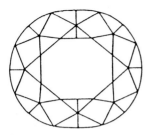

Weight: 48.63 CARATS
Cut/Shape: BRILLIANT/OVAL
Size: LENGTH 19.05 MM, WIDTH 31.75 MM
Colour: COLOURLESS
Owner/Location: UNKNOWN

A drawing of the Pigot diamond, whose whereabouts are not known. The gem was last seen in Turkey.

Britain's love affair with India lasted for more than two centuries. During this period, the British built railways and roads, and established the civil service. In return, they carried away gold-inlaid furniture, jewel-encrusted paintings and diamonds as big as apricots.

In 1755, George Pigot was appointed governor and commander-in-chief of Madras. It was he, who fought and defeated the French in 1758, maintaining the southern city of Madras as a part of the British Empire. But in 1775, he found himself faced with serious allegations from his council regarding Azim-ud-Daula, the Nawab of Arcot. It appears that the governor was willing to accept valuable gifts from the nawab in return for protecting his territory from invasion. In 1776, Pigot was condemned and the council had him arrested and imprisoned.

Among the presents that Pigot received was an oval-shaped diamond from Golconda, weighing 48.63 carats. Its water (transparency) was pure and brilliant. It had a small imperfection near the girdle, but this did not in any way detract from the sheer beauty of the gem. In 1777, Pigot bequeathed this 'bauble' to his sister and two brothers who, thirteen years later, unable to sell it in a normal manner, decided to dispose of the Pigot diamond in a unique way – by initiating a private act of parliament to sell it by lottery. In an official statement that was issued, the diamond was valued at around £30,000 and lottery tickets were sold for two guineas each.

The lucky winners of the lottery were part of a syndicate who later sold the diamond to a joint party consisting of a Mr Parker, of Parker & Birkett, Fleet Street, and the firm of Rundell & Co, who were subsequently appointed the crown jewellers of England.

In 1804, Napoleon Bonaparte declared himself emperor of France. Jewellers from all over Europe were excited on hearing the news that he

Napoleon Bonaparte, a prospective buyer of the Pigot, in his coronation robes in 1804.

was interested in buying gemstones for his coronation. Rundell & Co decided to dispatch the Pigot to France in the hope of catching the new emperor's attention. However, France and England were at war, so the difficult task of discreetly carrying the diamond to Napoleon was entrusted to a French employee of the firm, Philip Liebart. He deftly stitched the gem into the waistband of his underwear and proceeded to Paris. There he deposited it in a famous bank, Lafitte & Co, and soon after, it was shown to Napoleon. The emperor was enchanted with the stunning gem, but he became suspicious of the deal and was convinced that the diamond had been smuggled into France from England. His police immediately started their investigations and Liebart had to surreptitiously depart from Paris, leaving the diamond behind in the bank. It was only after Napoleon's defeat at the Battle of Waterloo in 1815 that Rundell & Co was able to recover the stone, which was returned to London in 1816.

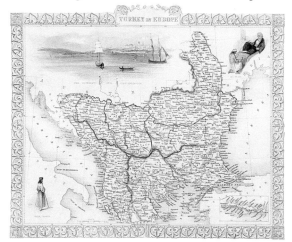

The Pigot might still be in Turkey, where the Pasha of Egypt presented it to Sultan Mahmud II in the early 19th century.

Rundell & Bridge, as the company was later called, tried to sell the Pigot again, by sending crystal models of it to prospective buyers. In 1822, Ali Pasha of Egypt fell in love with the gem and offered to pay for it in consignments of corn and cotton. The jewellers refused to accept commodities and finally a sum of £30,000 was agreed upon. The Pigot became the possession of Ali Pasha, who always carried it in a green silk purse secured to his girdle. He later presented the gem to Sultan Mahmud II of the Ottoman Empire in the hope of being appointed the governor of Egypt. In 1841, his wish was granted.

Today, neither the owner of the Pigot nor its whereabouts are known, but efforts to track it down continue. Every now and then a diamond with something in common with the famous gem appears, but the match is seldom perfect. Gemmologists and jewel lovers are still looking out for it in the hope that the historical diamond that disappeared amid the minarets of Turkey will, some day, resurface.

REGENT
A SLAVE'S BARGAIN

Weight: 140.50 CARATS
Cut/Shape: BRILLIANT/CUSHION
Size: LENGTH 25.40 MM, WIDTH 25.40 MM, DEPTH 18.00 MM
Colour: LIGHT BLUE TINT
Location: LOUVRE MUSEUM, PARIS

"Asleep and naked as an Indian lay, An honest factor stole a gem away; He pledged it to the Knight, the Knight had wit, So kept the diamond, and the rogue was bit." – It was believed that poet Alexander Pope was referring to Thomas Pitt in Epistle to Bathurst.

The ever-spreading web of the British Empire first reached India in the autumn of 1600, when a group of adventurous Englishmen set up the East India Company in Calcutta. With an initial capital of just £72,000, this little island in the English Channel soon enriched itself with treasures that were to colour its history in the coming centuries.

While on duty in India, many officers of the East India Company cultivated an interest in the rich heritage of the country. One such officer was Thomas Pitt, a merchant who because of his diligent efforts was made governor of Fort St George in Madras. During his tenure from 1698

Fort St George on the COROMANDEL Coast.
Belonging to the East India Company of England.

to 1709, Pitt, who had developed a keen interest in the diamond trade, acquired a beautiful 410-(old) carat diamond. This stone, discovered in 1701 in the deposits of the river Krishna (one of the mines in the Golconda region), was called the Pitt after him.

There are numerous accounts of how Pitt came to possess this fabulous gem. According to one story, a slave found the diamond and embedded it in his calf for safe keeping. He then ran off to sea and offered to give an English captain of a ship half the price of the diamond in exchange for his passage. The captain agreed, but later, consumed with greed, killed the slave and took possession of the gem. He then sold it to Pitt for £1,000.

When Pitt returned to England, rumours began to fly, suggesting that he had acquired the gem by unscrupulous means. Shortly after, Pitt wrote an open letter explaining how three years after his arrival in Madras, a well-known diamond merchant by the name of Jamchand had approached him with a collection of gems. Among these was a large stone of 410 (old) carats. Pitt had bargained with Jamchand till they had finally settled on a price of £20,000. The letter mentioned neither an Indian slave nor an English captain.

Camelford

The baronial crest of the House of Pitt.

While in Madras, Pitt had commissioned Isaac Abendana, a Dutch Jew, to make a model of the diamond in order to expedite its cutting at a later date in London. It was eventually cut over a period of two years into a brilliant by Joseph Cope, and the entire process cost £5,000. The newly-cut stone was cushion-shaped, and it now weighed 140.50 carats. Sparkling with a light blue tint, it possessed the purity of the finest Golconda gems and was probably the most beautifully cut of all the large diamonds of that time.

It is often said that a man with a fortune has no true friends. Pitt was convinced that someone was out to rob him of his beloved gem. Due to his perpetual restlessness, he wanted to sell off the diamond as quickly as possible, but this was easier said than done. He could not get any of the European royalty interested. In fact, when he offered it to Louis XIV of France in 1714, the jewelled royal hand waved him aside saying that France had spent all its money on war. The following year, Louis XV succeeded his great-grandfather to the throne. The new king of France was only five years old and till 1723, Philippe II, Duke of Orleans, was appointed the regent

The coronation crown of Louis XV in which the Regent diamond was set in 1722.

and managed the affairs of the state on his behalf. When Pitt offered the diamond to France again, the duke agreed to pay 2.5 million livres for it, and the stone's name changed from Pitt to Regent. The newly-acquired Regent joined the splendid crown jewels, and in 1721, it sparkled in the shoulder ornament of Louis XV when he attended a great banquet at Versailles Palace. The following year, it was set in his coronation crown. In 1725, on the occasion of Louis XV's marriage to Marie Leszcynska – the daughter of the exiled king of Poland – the Regent was seen again in a headband for the queen.

During the chaotic French Revolution of 1789, the crown jewels were taken from Versailles to the Garde Meuble, a building that served as a museum as well as a furniture shop. On the morning of September 17, 1792, the doors of the Garde Meuble opened to reveal that eleven closets, containing some of the great diamonds in the collection, including the Regent, had been

emptied by the revolutionaries during the previous night. Though this was a major loss to the country, at the time its citizens were too busy taking aristocrats to the guillotine to take much notice of the robbery. Luckily, after searching for a year, the most celebrated of the missing gems, the Regent, was found along with some other jewels in an attic in Paris.

All the jewels that were recovered became a part of the public treasury and facilitated several fiscal deals that were to finance the French army during the countless wars that followed. Napoleon Bonaparte came to power in 1799 and he had the Regent, which he considered to be a talisman, set in the hilt of his sword in 1802. In fact, by a strange irony, the

Napoleon Bonaparte (facing page), a great lover of fine jewels, was one of the owners of the Regent. He had the diamond set in the hilt of his sword (above) and considered it a lucky charm.

man who led Britain in the Napoleonic Wars was William Pitt, the great-grandson of Thomas Pitt.

The diamond passed through several royal hands and finally adorned the crown of Charles X, who ascended the throne of France in 1824. It stayed in the beautiful diadem till the marriage of Charles Louis Napoleon III to Eugénie María in 1853, when it was reset in a crown, the Greek, made for the empress. The setting was a groove from which the sparkling gem could be easily removed to use in some other piece of jewellery.

The Regent has thus been a part of the French Crown Jewels in one form or another since the early 18th century. Today, it is proudly displayed in the Galerie d'Apollon at the Louvre Museum and continues to be an abiding passion of the French. Its history has been preserved over the years through stories, fables and even films, which attempt to capture its awe-inspiring beauty. It is indeed a strange turn of events that an invaluable treasure unearthed in India should form part of the national heritage of a country nearly 11,000 km away.

The Louvre Museum (above), where the French Crown Jewels, including the Regent and the Sancy, are exhibited in the Galerie d'Apollon. In 1824, Charles X (facing page) became the sovereign of France and had the Regent set in his crown, where it remained till 1853.

SANCY

AN IRRESISTABLE BOOTY

Weight: 55.23 CARATS
Cut/Shape: ROSE/OVAL-PEAR
Size: LENGTH 25.70 MM, WIDTH 20.60 MM, DEPTH 14.30 MM
Colour: PURE WHITE
Location: LOUVRE MUSEUM, PARIS

"A greate and ryche jewell of golde called the 'Myrror of Greate Brytayne' conteyninge one verie fayre table dyamonde.... twoe other lardge dyamondes ... garnyshed wyth smalle dyamandes, twoe rounde perles fixed and one fayre dyamonde cutt in fawcettis, bought of Sauncey."
– Inventory of the Jewels in the Tower of London, 1605.

From the earliest times, diamonds have been looked upon as symbols of success and prosperity, whether they have glorified a god, embellished a monarch, or decorated a lover. Rulers have lost their thrones because of them, empires have built their wealth on them, and ordinary men have made millions by finding and selling them. These precious stones have been revered as artefacts, owing to their beauty and wonderful ability to last forever, perfect and untouched by the ravages of time. Only the most distressing circumstances such as war, natural disaster, or personal misfortune would cause a reluctant owner to relinquish such a treasure. In the event of such calamities, diamonds have been known to buy armies, positions and favours, their iridescent fire holding a strange fascination for every king or collector who acquired them.

The Sancy is one such diamond that has changed hands many times. This 55.23-carat stone, found in Golconda, is cut in a traditional Indian style in an oval-pear shape with facets on both sides. It is pure white and nearly flawless, with only a small imperfection near the surface.

The fate of the Sancy has been unusual when compared to other diamonds, in that it has often provided guarantee for raising troops, aided monarchs in protecting their kingdoms, and caused the sacrifice of a man's life. Though its early history in India is ambiguous, it is known that the gem began its long journey along the caravan routes to the West till it finally reached Constantinople. Here, it was bought by Nicholas Harlay de Sancy who named the shimmering stone after himself and thus, became immortalised in diamond history.

Nicholas Harlay de Sancy sold his eponymous diamond to King James I in 1604.

M.re NICOLAS DE HARLAY CHEVALIER SEIG.r DE SANCY BARON DE MAVLE &.c. COLONEL GENERAL DES SVISSES. aage de 35. ans.

Van Moalins f. 1 6 5 3

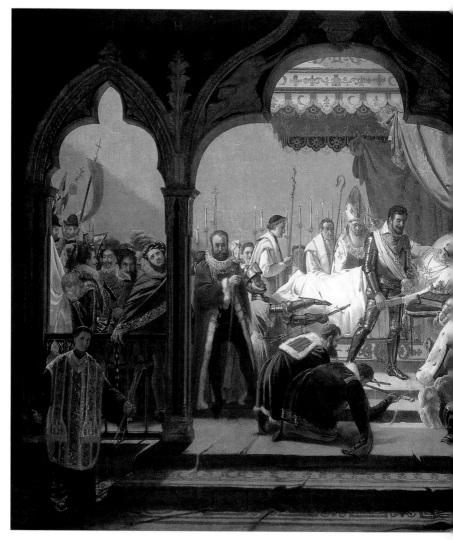

A painting depicting Henry of Navarre receiving the Attributes of Monarchy from the dying Henry III. Nicholas Harlay de Sancy often pledged his valuable gem to aid both these monarchs.

De Sancy returned to France in 1589, the year of the French rebellion. King Henry III needed quick capital to raise troops and ordered Sancy to pawn his valuable diamond in exchange for the required sum. In return for this favour, he was appointed colonel-in-chief of a twelve thousand-strong regiment of Swiss soldiers. In the same year, Henry III was fatally wounded

by a Dominican monk and on his deathbed, he nominated Henry of Navarre as his successor. Henry of Navarre founded the Bourbon dynasty, and soon after ascending the throne as Henry IV, he appointed Sancy the Superintendent of Finance. Using the power of this coveted position, Sancy redeemed the precious gem, pledging it time and again over the next few years to aid his monarch.

As the rebellion intensified, the financial situation in France deteriorated and Sancy decided to send the diamond to his brother in London for safe keeping. He entrusted it in great secrecy to a faithful servant but despite all precautions, word of the gem's impending journey leaked out. As the man travelled through the French countryside, he was waylaid and killed. As soon as Sancy heard this news, he set off for the forest where the murder had occurred. Suspecting that his faithful servant might have swallowed the diamond to save it from the thieves, he ordered that a post-mortem be done. Sure enough, the gem was there and he recovered it without any further delay.

After this, Sancy tried to sell the diamond to several monarchs in Europe but was unsuccessful. Once again, he decided to send the stone to London. The year was 1604 and Sancy's cousin, who was the French ambassador in London, succeeded in selling the diamond to King James I. In the same year, James I designated several jewels to be part of the crown jewels in an attempt to safeguard them for posterity. However, his son and heir, Charles I, found himself enmeshed in financial difficulties from the beginning of his beleaguered reign. The situation worsened, and in 1644, he sent his wife, Queen Henrietta Maria, daughter of Henry IV of France, to her homeland with a box containing some of the crown jewels that included the Sancy.

Queen Henrietta Maria tried to pawn this gem in a deal with the Netherlands but was unsuccessful, and finally managed to pledge the jewels to the Duke of Épernon instead. As time went on and the pledge remained unredeemed, the duke sold the Sancy as well as the table-cut Mirror of Portugal diamond to Cardinal Jules Mazarin.

Cardinal Mazarin, First Minister of the Crown, was a keen collector of art and diamonds in 17th-century France. He was said to love precious gems even more than his god, and in his will he left his beautiful collection of 18 large diamonds, including the Sancy, to the Crown, requesting that the gems be known as the Mazarin diamonds. The Sancy, which was the largest of the Mazarins, came to be known as Mazarin I and joined the royal riches as one of the crown jewels of France. In 1722, it was superbly set along with the Regent diamond in the beautiful diadem made for the coronation of Louis XV. The king also wore the Sancy set in a brooch on his hat, and his queen, Marie Leszcynska, wore it as a pendant. During the reign of the next king, Louis XVI, much of the crown jewellery was taken apart and reset as favoured by his wife, Queen Marie Antoinette.

This idyllic period for the French royalty came to a rude and abrupt end with the outbreak of the French Revolution in 1789, which finally led to the execution of Louis XVI and his queen in 1793. In this time of strife and unrest, the crown jewels were removed from the palace of Versailles to the Garde Meuble for safe keeping. However, their safety was short-lived and in September 1792, the treasure was looted by the revolutionaries. In an anxious search that ensued, some of the crown jewels were recovered – the Regent was found in an attic, the Great Hortensia in the roof of a house, and another heap of jewels was found buried under a tree in a leafy avenue in Paris by the police who were tipped off by a sixteen-year-old fortune teller. There was no trace of the Mirror of Portugal or the Sancy.

After a short interval, the Sancy mysteriously reappeared in the possession of the Marquis of Iranda in Madrid, who received it as a pawn for supplying horses to the French army. He in turn pledged it to pay the Spanish cavalry, and soon after, the Sancy became the property of Queen Maria Louisa of Spain. Seven years after the theft at the Garde Meuble, the famous Spanish artist Goya painted a portrait of the queen wearing an amber-rose gown of spun gold and the Sancy as an ornament.

In 1828, the diamond changed hands again and became the property of Prince Nicholas Demidoff of Russia. After his death, his son Paul married a Finnish lady, Aurora Stjernvall, in 1836, and presented the Sancy to her.

The gem probably stayed in the Demidoff family till 1865, when an article in the *Illustrated London News* dated March 11, 1865 read: "…the celebrated Sancy diamond which has been purchased for £20,000 by Messrs R. and S. Garrard & Co of the Haymarket for Sir Jamsetjee Jejeebhoy, the great Parsee merchant of Bombay…." It is rumoured that the stone did not stay in Bombay for long and it was soon sold to Maharaja Bhupindra Singh of Patiala who was an avid collector of fine diamonds. An apocryphal tale describes him making an exotic appearance at the 1911 Delhi Durbar, held for the Prince of Wales, walking through the pale caramel-coloured hall wearing his brocade coat, jewelled sword, and the Sancy in the silk folds of his ice blue turban.

In 1892, the Sancy officially resurfaced when William Waldorf Astor bought it for his wife. It soon passed to their daughter-in-law, Lady Astor, the first woman member of Parliament in the House of Commons in England, and she wore it mounted in a glittering tiara. In 1978, the fourth Viscount Astor sold the Sancy jointly to the Banque de France and Musées de France for an alleged sum of $1 million. The celebrated gem is now on display along with the Regent diamond in the Louvre Museum in Paris.

Engraved by D. J. Pound from a Photograph by Mr Barahjee Jamsetjee of Bombay.

THE LATE

SIR JAMSETJEE JEEJEEBHOY, BART

THE DRAWING ROOM PORTRAIT GALLERY OF EMINENT PERSONAGES
Presented with the Illustrated News of the World
THE LONDON JOINT STOCK NEWSPAPER COMPANY LIMITED

The Sancy made a short sojourn to India in 1865 when it was purchased for £20,000 by a London jeweller for the great Parsi merchant, Sir Jamsetjee Jeejeebhoy.

The Sancy and the Regent seem to be linked by a common destiny. After being stolen from the Garde Meuble on the same fateful night in September 1792, they went their separate ways to finally meet again in the hallowed Parisian museum.

HOPE
THE CURSE OF BLUE FIRE

Weight: 45.52 CARATS
Cut/Shape: MODIFIED BRILLIANT/CUSHION
Size: LENGTH 21.78 MM, WIDTH 25.60 MM, DEPTH 12.00 MM
Colour: SAPPHIRE BLUE
Location: SMITHSONIAN INSTITUTION, WASHINGTON DC

"She blamed the diamond; and as one woman to another, she begged me to throw it away and break its spell." – Evalyn Walsh McLean, referring to a letter sent to her by actress Mary Yohé, a previous owner of the Hope.

Of all the gemstones in the world, diamonds have been particularly attributed with potent occult powers. Indians believe that these intrinsic energies can either take the destiny of the owner to soaring heights, or send it plummeting into abysmal doom. While a spotless stone is said to make a monarch of a man, a flawed diamond is considered by some to be a harbinger of ill luck.

This belief is reflected in the story of the much-maligned Hope, a blue diamond, which left behind a bewildering trail of misfortune as it passed from one owner to the next.

The Hope was unearthed in the Kollur mine in Golconda. Its rare sapphire blue colour is the result of the replacement of some carbon atoms within the diamond by a concentration of boron atoms. Due to the boron, the stone becomes a semiconductor and the absorption of light in the red part of the spectrum leads to the unusual blue colour. Though it is an unsymmetrical stone because of its mixed cut, the Hope has a special prismatic fire, making it one of the most beautiful diamonds in the world.

This lustrous stone came into the possession of the French jeweller and gem merchant Jean-Baptiste Tavernier while he was in India. It was the most bewitching diamond in his collection of stones from the East and soon after his return to France in 1668, he sold it to Louis XIV. The gem, with a recorded early weight of 112.53 Florentine carats (about 110.50 metric carats), first came to be known as Tavernier Blue and was bought by the king along with 45 large and 1,122 smaller diamonds. According to some sources, Tavernier, the first known owner of the controversial Hope, ended his days penniless and was killed by a pack of wild dogs.

In 1673, Louis XIV, preferring brilliance to size, ordered his lapidary and goldsmith, Sieur Pitau, to recut the Hope into a glittering 67.12-carat heart.

Louis XIV bought the bewitching Hope diamond from Jean-Baptiste Tavernier around 1668.

Louis XV wearing the Order of the Golden Fleece, an ornament which held the blue Hope diamond.

The indigo blue Hope was now known as the Blue Diamond of the Crown, but this rather long name of the gem soon got shortened to the French Blue. It was worn by Louis XIV as a pendant suspended on a ribbon. In 1749, Louis XV commissioned his court jeweller, Andre Jacquemin, to craft the French Blue into a piece of ceremonial jewellery, the Order of the Golden Fleece (Toison D'or). The diamond remained in this ornament for many years and is said to have delighted Queen Marie Antoinette during the reign of her husband Louis XVI. It has been suggested that she was 'cursed' because of her ownership of the diamond, resulting in her imprisonment and violent execution.

During the turbulent period of the French Revolution, the crown jewels were removed to the Garde Meuble. In September 1792, the French Blue was part of the loot – that also included the Regent – carried off by the marauding revolutionaries, after which it was considered to be lost forever.

Almost two decades later, an irregularly cut 45.52-carat blue diamond suddenly surfaced in London causing much speculation about its identity. During this time it was said to have been cut by Wilhelm Fals, a Dutch lapidary. His son Hendrick reportedly stole the gem from his father, who died of heartbreak at the son's misbehaviour. Unable to withstand the guilt, Hendrick is supposed to have committed suicide.

The gem was bought by Henry Philip Hope of a famous banking family who owned Hope & Co. It was thereafter called the Hope and it retained this name even as its owners kept changing. In keeping with the diamond's allegedly sinister antecedents, the banking company encountered financial difficulties and by 1813 it was on the verge of closure. Henry Hope died unmarried in 1839, leaving his fortune to his three nephews. The eldest, Henry Thomas Hope, acquired the coveted diamond from his uncle's estate. He died at a relatively early age of fifty-four, and his widow later married Henry Pelham-Clinton. She kept the gem in her custody and gave this quintessential heirloom in 1887 to her grandson on the condition that he add the name Hope to his Pelham-Clinton. He accepted this term and became Lord Henry Francis Pelham-Clinton Hope. Six years later, in 1893, he found himself deep in debt because of his love of gambling, and the following year he married an American actress, Mary Yohé, who supported them. However, by 1898 Lord Francis once again owed money to his creditors, so he made a contract with L M Lowenstein & Co for the sale of the Hope. This was not an easy task. His sisters and brother opposed the sale in court and the matter had to be abandoned.

After much tribulation, Lord Francis was at last allowed to dispose of the Hope in 1901. He reportedly sold it to Adolf Weil of Hatton Garden, London's famous diamond quarter, and the gem took leave of the family that had retained and carried forward its name. Another account mentions that the diamond was bought by a New York jeweller.

At this point, the story of the Hope takes bizarre twists and turns. It is said that it went on to become the possession of a French jeweller, Jacques Colet, who went insane and committed suicide. Another of its owners was Ivan Kanitowsky, a Russian prince who presented it to Mademoiselle

Lorens Laduc, a Folies-Bergère actress. She was shot as she wore the gem on stage the very next day and the unfortunate prince was later killed by the Russian revolutionaries.

Alternatively, it is also believed that the beautiful blue stone attracted the interest of a New York dealer, Simon Frankel, from the firm of Joseph Frankel's Sons, who paid Adolf Weil £33,000 for it. Frankel later sold it to Salomon Habib, an agent representing Abdul Hamid II – the sultan of Turkey (also known as 'Abdul the Damned') – in this transaction. The sultan, a great collector of beautiful jewellery and lovely women, gave the diamond to his mistress. The beleaguered gem once again proved to be a harbinger of misfortune as the lady shot herself and the sultan was deposed in 1909.

The Hope was in the market once again and this time it was bought by the Parisian diamond merchant, C H Rosenau, who sold it to Pierre Cartier, the famous jeweller. Cartier was responsible for the sale of the Hope to the well-known socialite Evalyn Walsh McLean of Washington DC. While she and her husband were on their honeymoon in Paris in 1910, he took the Hope to their hotel, hoping to tempt her to buy the shimmering gem. She politely declined saying that she did not like the setting. However, she had heard tales about the notorious diamond, and at that meeting, mentioned to Cartier that objects considered unlucky by others actually proved lucky for her. He went to America later that year with the intention of persuading McLean to add the Hope to her magnificent collection of diamonds.

The Hope in a necklace designed by Pierre Cartier. In spite of the legendary curse associated with it, the diamond attracted countless buyers such as socialite Evalyn Walsh McLean.

The Thickness.

The upper Part

The under Part

Top to bottom: *Three views of the violet-blue gem sold by Tavernier to Louis XIV, from which the Hope was cut. A drawing of the Hope from the 1839 catalogue of Henry Philip Hope's gem collection.*

Cartier reset the stone in a new necklace and it was he, it is alleged, who created the story of the lovely blue being a jinxed stone that had an eternal tryst with catastrophe. McLean toyed with the idea for a few months and finally agreed to buy the Hope for £180,000, to be paid in instalments.

Although McLean loved wearing the Hope and refused to believe in its fabled curse, her life was beset with tragedy once she acquired it. Her brother died early; her eldest son was run over by a car when he was only nine years old. She divorced her husband, who later died in a mental institution. Her daughter died from an overdose of sleeping pills at twenty-five, and the following year, in 1947, crushed by the weight of her grief, McLean died of pneumonia at sixty. The ill luck persisted and her granddaughter too died at a young age of twenty-five.

McLean died on a Saturday and the executors of her will needed a safe place to keep her sizeable collection of jewellery over the weekend. She was known to hide it around her house for safe keeping and the Hope sometimes spent quiet intervals secreted in the upholstery of an armchair. By the time all her jewellery had been collected, banks had closed and permission was sought from the Federal Bureau of Investigation to place it in one of their safes.

Though McLean bequeathed her fortune to her grandchildren, they were not fortunate enough to enjoy this wealth. Two years after her death, her jewels had to be sold to pay debts and claims against the estate. In 1949, the famous New York jeweller, Harry Winston, purchased McLean's jewellery collection, including the Hope, for over a million dollars. Winston too was a disbeliever and in spite of the legendary curse, travelled around the world with the diamond.

In 1958, Winston presented the historic diamond to the Smithsonian Institution in Washington. Whether or not the Hope is an accursed gem, it is now inextricably linked with the tragic lives of many of its possessors.

NASSAK
THE PESHWA'S TREASURE

Weight: 43.38 CARATS
Cut/Shape: EMERALD/TRIANGLE
Colour: COLOURLESS
Owner: ROBERT MOUAWAD, PARIS

A glass model of the Nassak diamond, one of the principal gems taken away by the British when they confiscated the Peshwa's jewels in 1818.

Nasik, situated near the source of the river Godavari in the state of Maharashtra, is a sacred place for Hindus and its association with the gods Rama and Shiva is evident in the mosaic of temples that dot its dusky landscape. The town is identified with the story of Rama's exile and wandering, and with his wife Sita's abduction by Ravana. It is said to have received its name from an episode in the Hindu epic Ramayana, where the nose (*nasika*) of the ogress Shurpanaka was cut off by Rama's brother, Laxmana.

Drawn by C Delidou from a sketch by Capt. Meadows Taylor.

Engraved by J. Smith.

A view of Nasik, the town which gave the Nassak diamond its name.

The chequered history of the Nassak diamond begins in this revered town from which it seems to have derived its name. This Golconda stone, another example of the earlier wealth of Indian temples, is alleged to have been the eye of a Shiva idol in one of the shrines in Nasik. The diamond was said to have been embedded there by a Maratha chief, but as time passed and the Maratha Empire began to crumble, it was stolen. Passing through several hands, it finally became the property of the ruling Peshwa, Bajirao II. In 1818, in an impatient bid to strengthen their empire, the British fought and vanquished the Peshwas, storming their timbered palace. Emeralds, diamonds, pale pink rubies, drinking cups of gold and coffers of iridescent pearls dazzled the imperious Englishmen who ransacked chests after chests of treasures. The hapless Peshwa tried his best to conceal the Nassak diamond but Colonel Briggs, in charge of the plunder, smoothly confiscated the prized booty along with all the other jewels, and took it to Governor-General Warren Hastings who was commander-in-chief of the forces in India.

The Nassak was supposedly the eye of a Shiva idol in a temple in Nasik, such as this one.

Hastings, a purveyor of 'English justice', handed over the beautiful gem to the East India Company, which held the enviable position of taking into its possession almost anything of value found in the richest colony of the empire.

Following routine procedures, the East India Company had the Nassak sent to England. At that time, the stone weighed 89 carats, was triangular in shape, and had been cut in an old Indian style that did nothing for its brilliance.

The Nassak was received by George III who ceremoniously passed it on to the distinguished firm of Rundell & Bridge, the crown jewellers. Rundell & Bridge were aware of the difference that finer faceting would make to the Nassak. This task was so skilfully carried out that the resulting gem was reduced to 80.59 carats, a loss of a little less than 10 per cent. In July 1831, during the time of a national financial depression, the Nassak was bought by

Before its journey to England, the Nassak was temporarily in the custody of Warren Hastings.

Painted by Sir Joshua Reynolds, P.R.A.   Engraved by H. Robinson.

RT HON.BLE WARREN HASTINGS. L.L.D. F.R.S. &c.&c.

Warren Hastings

FISHER, SON & C.º LONDON, 1836.

The first Marquess of Westminster bought the Nassak in 1837.

Emmanuel Brothers, the London jewellers, for an astonishingly low sum of £7,200. This was a third of the gem's estimated price and the new owners were in all likelihood proud to have made a sterling investment for a mere pittance.

Subsequently, the glittering Nassak came up for auction at Willis's Rooms in London on July 20, 1837. *The Times* reported that the room was "filled with all the cognoscenti in precious stones and all the principal dealers, attracted by the announcement that the celebrated 'Nassak' diamond, the 'Arcot' diamonds and a variety of most other costly diamonds and pearls, the property of the late Mr Bridge, of Ludgate Hill, would be sold by auction by Mr Sharp. The sale commenced at 3 o'clock." The person who purchased the Nassak, as well as the two pear-shaped Arcot diamonds, was the first Marquess of Westminster.

On the occasion of Queen Victoria's eighteenth birthday reception, soon after her ascension to the throne of England in 1837, the marquess wore the lustrous Nassak in the hilt of his dress-sword. The diamond remained in his family till 1926, when the second Marquess of Westminster sold it to the famous Parisian jeweller, Georges Mauboussin.

Mauboussin tried to sell the Nassak in Europe, but his efforts were in vain. In order to explore a new market, he dispatched the gem to the United States of America, designating it as an 'artistic antique', meant for display. This caused a furore among American jewellery dealers who knew that he had cleverly labelled it as an antique to avoid excise duties.

The Nassak was then sent back to Paris where, in 1940, it was purchased by the New York jewellery firm Harry Winston Inc. It then made its second voyage to America. Winston had it recut in New York to an emerald cut, and it now weighed 43.38 carats, retaining its triangular shape. He sold it to another New York jeweller, who in turn sold it in 1944 to Mrs William M Leeds. She had it set in a ring embellished with two tapered baguettes.

The Taylor-Burton was the first to be sold for a spectacular price, followed by the Nassak.

On April 16, 1970, the Nassak came up for auction again, this time at the Parke-Bernet Galleries Inc in New York. In a matter of minutes, the gem was bought by Edward Hand of Greenwich, Connecticut, for a sum of $500,000. Hand, who was once married to the famous tennis player of the fifties, Gussie Moran, said, "I think it was a bargain. I was prepared to go as high as $750,000." This purchase made history in diamond sales at that time, as the Nassak had been sold for a price that was the second highest ever paid for a gem. The highest was paid by Richard Burton when he bought the fabulous 69.40-carat pear-shaped diamond for his wife Elizabeth Taylor only a year earlier. The Taylor-Burton diamond was the first to break the million-dollar mark and it was bought for a grand sum of $1.05 million.

It was only after the sixties that the sales of gemstones began to realise spectacular prices. The figures recorded at one auction were completely eclipsed by the knock of the hammer at another. From a purely pecuniary perspective, the Nassak too finally broke away from the disappointing sale prices that it had attracted in the past and came into its own as a superlative gem of great value in the intensely competitive auction of 1970.

Later, the gem was bought jointly by Bulgari, the famous jewellery firm of Italy, and J & S S De Young, the Boston estate goods firm. In 1977, they sold it to the king of Saudi Arabia, Khalid bin Abdulaziz Al-Saud. It was later sold to Robert Mouawad, head of the international Mouawad company that specialises in fine jewellery. This firm was founded in 1890 in Lebanon by his grandfather. Today, Mouawad owns one of the most important collections of historically famous diamonds that includes the Indore Pears, Jubilee, Queen of Holland and Tereschenko.

After its great journeys all over the world, the Nassak's association with India has become almost chimerical and yet, to any observer of history, it remains an abiding symbol of the plunder that divested India of so much of its wealth under the insatiable canopy of the British Raj.

DARYA-I-NOOR
THE PRIDE OF IRAN

Weight: APPROX 185 CARATS

Cut/Shape: TABLE/RECTANGLE

Size: LENGTH 29.50 MM, WIDTH 41.40 MM, DEPTH 12.15 MM

Colour: PALE PINK

Location: NATIONAL JEWELS MUSEUM, TEHRAN

Dreamy pink diamonds, especially prized because of their rarity, were made into a fashion statement by the New York jeweller Ralph Esmerian in the early 20th century.

The most celebrated diamonds of all time came from the sand and soil of India, though, today, Indian sources are said to have dwindled. While all these gems are wrapped in a cloak of mystery and intrigue, the Darya-i-Noor, or 'Sea of Light', is probably one of the few diamonds to have repeatedly invited speculation about its identity.

This pale pink, shimmering stone was discovered in the rich alluvial deposits of Golconda and it possesses a unique limpidity that is characteristic of the finest Indian diamonds. It is a table-cut stone and its pavilion consists of large step facets. One of these bears an inscription in Persian, "The Sultan, Sahib Qiram, Fath Ali Shah, Qajar 1250" (AD 1834, the year of his death). The weight of this fabulous gem has never been accurately determined probably because it has been variously set as an armlet, a brooch and an aigrette. However, it is estimated to be about 185 carats, making it the largest pink diamond known to man. The gem is now set in a frame with 457 diamonds and 24 rubies, and can be seen in the National Jewels Museum in Tehran. The beautiful pink colour does not stem from a trace element, as in the case of yellow (nitrogen) or blue (boron) diamonds, but is the probable result of graining and structural complexities. The world output of pink diamonds being so low, these lovely stones are highly desirable and attract record prices whenever they are sold.

The story of the Darya-i-Noor begins with an invaluable account in Jean-Baptiste Tavernier's *Travels in India*, in which he describes a magnificent diamond that he had seen in one of the mines in the Golconda region. In 1642, he drew a diagram of this stone, recorded its weight as 242 carats, and referred to it as the Great Table diamond.

Since then, the Great Table has been believed to be lost, but gemmologists and collectors the world over find it hard to accept that

The luminous pink Darya-i-Noor is set in a frame with 457 diamonds and 24 rubies and is in Tehran.

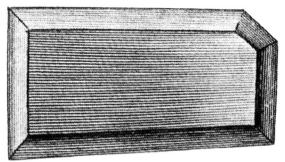

Tavernier's drawing of the Great Table diamond (left). A painting (below) by Robert Smirke, depicting a meeting between Fath Ali Shah and Sir Harford Jones Brydges, English envoy to the Persian court and Luft Ali Khan's agent in the sale of the Darya-i-Noor.

a stone of such size and beauty could disappear without a trace. In fact, experts often assumed that it had been stolen and broken up into smaller pieces, or renamed by various owners. Coincidentally, this assumption was proved right by the following series of events. In 1966, the Birks Family Foundation made available a grant, which enabled three gemmologists of the Royal Ontario Museum in Toronto to study and certify the crown jewels of Iran. The highlight of their work was a startling revelation about a particular stone in the collection. This gem, called the Darya-i-Noor, possessed a rare pink luminosity which perfectly matched the legendary Great Table diamond. The lost link to the historical diamond was on its way to be found. The Canadian gemmologists concluded that the Darya-i-Noor was indeed a cleavage of the Great Table.

How was it that a stone unearthed in India had become the prized possession of the crown jewels of Iran? Since Nadir Shah's sack of Delhi in 1739, it is generally accepted that several priceless and famous diamonds found their way into the treasury in Tehran. Two of the world's most stunning diamonds, the Darya-i-Noor and the Taj-i-Mah, both of Indian origin, are still a focal point of the collection.

Another piece of the jigsaw was provided by the introduction to *The Dynasty of the Kajars* by Sir Harford Jones Brydges, who was appointed envoy to the court of Persia from 1807 to 1811 during the reign of Fath Ali Shah. Before this, in 1791, Brydges was authorised by Luft Ali Khan, the last ruler of the Zend dynasty, to act as an agent in the sale of the Darya-i-Noor in order to raise money for his war against the Qajar chief, Aga Mohammed Khan. During this time, Brydges got the rare opportunity to examine the magnificent stone in the treasury. He described the Darya-i-Noor as a table diamond with a pale pink sparkle, validating Tavernier's description of the beautiful gem. The only discrepancy lay in the weight of the diamond. Mirza Jaunee,

The Noor-ul-Ain is set in a dazzling tiara created for Empress Farah Diba of Iran in 1958.

a lapidary in Ali Khan's court, reported to Brydges that it weighed a little over 176 carats, whereas Tavernier's records about the gem stated that it weighed 242 carats. The Canadian gemmologists sieved through the details till they found the reason for this disparity. They suggested that the mistake was probably an oversight and the weight reported to Brydges should have been a little over 176 '*mangelins*' and not 'carats'. A *mangelin* is an old Indian weight for gems and one *mangelin* is approximately 1.40 carats. Another link in the long chain of events fell into place.

However, if the Great Table and the Darya-i-Noor are one and the same as suggested by Brydges, the diamond called Darya-i-Noor that we see today is certainly different from the one described by Tavernier. The present Darya-i-Noor is noticeably shorter than the Great Table drawn by Tavernier. Also, the gem had not been inscribed when Brydges inspected it in Persia. Based on the assumption that in the East, gems in general, and diamonds in particular, were chosen for their size rather than for brilliance, the Canadian gemmologists inferred that the Darya-i-Noor had been involved in an accident which split it. This probably occurred around 1834, the year inscribed on the stone. It is important to clarify here, that a diamond's hardness is not to be confused with fragility, for if a brilliantly cut diamond was to drop to the ground with force, it would split if the impact occurred at the point of its cleavage. Also if the Darya-i-Noor was in fact a part of the Great Table, what happened to the remainder?

This mystery was solved when another pink diamond, the Noor-ul-Ain, or 'Light of the Eye', was found in the Iranian Crown Jewels. The Noor-ul-Ain is estimated to be around 60 carats and possesses a slight imperfection, which presumably occurred when the stone split from the larger Darya-i-Noor in the diamond workshop of the Golestan Palace in Tehran. This slightly drop-shaped oval matched the colour and limpidity of the Darya-i-Noor exactly and was the centrepiece of a fabulous tiara made by Harry Winston, the New York jeweller, for Empress Farah Diba to wear at her wedding in 1958. The tiara also has blue, pink, yellow and colourless diamonds among which is a yellow 10-carat pear-shaped stone.

However, the total weight of the Darya-i-Noor and the Noor-ul-Ain surpassed that of the Great Table and did not take into account any loss during cutting. Experiments to solve this puzzle resumed with renewed vigour and it was proved that Tavernier's report stating the weight as 242 carats was incorrect. At last, the identity of the Darya-i-Noor had been unequivocally established on the firmament of diamond history.

The Darya-i-Noor, which adorned the military cap of the last Shah of Iran at his coronation in 1967, has survived the weathering of time; its fragile existence often threatened by the ravages of war and accident.

The Golestan Palace in Tehran contained workshops where diamond cutting was carried out. It is presumed that the accident that split the Noor-ul-Ain from the Darya-i-Noor occurred in one of these.

WITTELSBACH
THE SPANISH DOWRY

A glass model of the sapphire blue Wittelsbach. The stone's breathtaking colour, which can only be compared with that of the Hope, makes it one of the most precious gems of all time.

Weight: 35.50 CARATS
Cut/Shape: BRILLIANT/OVAL
Size: LENGTH 26.00 MM, WIDTH 29.00 MM, DEPTH 8.29 MM
Colour: SAPPHIRE BLUE
Owner/Location: UNKNOWN

Once in a while, a diamond makes an appearance that causes the world to hold its breath. One such stone is the famous blue Wittelsbach that reappeared in 1962, nearly thirty years after it had slipped into anonymity.

The Wittelsbach is considered to be one of the most famous diamonds in history and has been especially sought after for its exceptional blue colour. This sparkling stone weighs 35.50 carats and is intricately cut with 50 facets, arranged in an irregular pattern. The stone is flawless except for a few fine scratches that have probably been caused due to its constant resetting and use.

Diamonds of all colours have been regarded as symbols of power and desire. Jean–Baptiste Tavernier introduced coloured diamonds, which he discovered during his travels to India, to the courts of Europe during the 17th century. These gems added a new sunburst of colours to the existing spectrum of coloured stones. It is impossible to compare the rarest of coloured diamonds – red, blue and green – to their coloured stone counterparts, such as ruby, sapphire and emerald. Diamonds possess a level of brilliance and dispersion (separation of white light into spectral colours) which coloured gems do not have.

Natural fancy blue diamonds are among the rarest of all coloured diamonds. Usually, blue diamonds have a steely cast that covers a vast range of tones. Therefore, when an intense blue gem surfaces, it is truly extraordinary. Blue diamonds in the rough are generally uneven in shape and have an irregular colour zoning. It is only the dexterity of the cutter that can fully realise the potential of a particular stone, and so, any natural fancy coloured diamond in the world market inevitably fetches record high prices. These priceless offerings of the earth possess a certain elusive glamour, which makes them seem magical and unique. Aptly described as a "drop of frozen light", a diamond, in spite of countless

Infanta Margareta Teresa was given the Wittelsbach by her father, Philip IV of Spain, at her wedding.

mishaps and misadventures, remains inviolate and imperishable, casting its glittering spell on mankind through the ages.

The recorded history of this intense blue stone, which must be from Golconda, drifts through several marbled palaces of Europe and begins in Spain. The Wittelsbach was a gift from Philip IV of Spain to his fifteen-year-old daughter, the Infanta Margareta Teresa, when she married Emperor Leopold I of Austria in 1664. Unfortunately, all records of the gem prior to this wedding were lost when the Madrid archives were destroyed during the Spanish Civil War of 1936-39. After Margareta's untimely death in 1675, her jewels passed to her husband, Leopold, who had an inventory made of them. The entry about the Wittelsbach reads, "Diamond ornament... consisting of... a large brooch with a Great Blue Diamond in the centre, to which belongs a bow-shaped jewel set with rubies."

Leopold later remarried twice, but gave his Spanish inheritance to his third wife, Empress Eleonore Magdalena. She lived longer than the emperor and when she died in 1720, she bequeathed the Great Blue Diamond to her granddaughter, the Archduchess Maria Amelia.

When Amelia married Charles Albert, the Bavarian Crown Prince, in 1722, the burnished blue embarked on the next stage of its journey as part of her dowry. It later came to be designated the family diamond of the Wittelsbachs, the ruling house of Bavaria, and retained this esteemed position till the abdication of the last king in 1918.

The extravagant nuptial festivities over, the father of the crown prince, Elector Maximilian Emmanuel, found himself in a financial quagmire. He pawned the Wittelsbach diamond along with a golden dinner service to a banker named Oppenheim, but the Elector died soon after and the task of compensating this amount fell on his son and heir.

The last king of Bavaria to wear the Wittelsbach was Louis III who was in power till 1918, when Germany became a republic. He died in 1921, and the beautiful stone, which had been the family heirloom for nearly two centuries, adorned the king for the very last time during his funeral.

A few years after the First World War, the riches of the Wittelsbachs were managed by a trust that compensated the members of the erstwhile royal family. But after the family found themselves in a state of financial distress, the state agreed that a certain part of the crown jewels of the Wittelsbachs could be sold. The coveted role of auctioneers of the Bavarian Crown Jewels went to Christie's who announced the sale in 1931. The Wittelsbach was bought for £5,400 by a mysterious buyer under an assumed name, Thorp.

From then on the trail of the Wittelsbach is obscure. In 1962, Joseph Komkommer, a luminary of the Belgium diamond industry, was consulted about an old stone that was to be reset. When he lifted the fiery blue gem

Charles Albert, the Bavarian Crown Prince, whose wife Amelia brought the Wittelsbach in her dowry.

out of its creamy box, he realised immediately that he was holding in his palm a precious relic. With the help of his son, Jacques Komkommer, he authenticated the diamond as the lost Wittelsbach. He then formed a syndicate of diamond merchants from Belgium and the United States of America and purchased the beautiful gem for £180,000. Apparently, the Wittelsbach had been part of an estate held in trust and the identity of the true owner was kept a secret. In 1964, the stone was bought by a private collector, and after its many alliances with royalty and international gem moguls, a more private phase in its history began.

Weight: 70.21 CARATS
Cut/Shape: MODIFIED BRILLIANT/ANTIQUE TRIANGLE
Size: DIAMETER 26.10 MM, DEPTH 13.43 MM
Colour: BLUE TINT
Owner/Location: UNKNOWN

According to legend, the diamond was set as an eye of a temple deity. If indeed it was a part of an idol, the whereabouts of the other eye will always remain a mystery.

In 1875, the Prince of Wales (the future Edward VII) sailed to India for a royal tour of the colony. The worldly son of Queen Victoria enjoyed the hospitality of devoted brocade-clad maharajas who took him on wild hunts in privately-owned forests and invited him to flamboyant parties where champagne flowed freely. A delighted prince returned to England on board the HMS *Osborne*, its hold weighed down with beds of gold, baths of silver, and casks of diamonds, rubies and emeralds. An observer of the tour is said to have remarked that diamonds seemed as plentiful in India as blackberries in England.

Since time immemorial, India was looked upon as a land of milk and honey, rich with rivers of diamonds and palaces decorated with gold. Fabulous temple treasures sparkled in the flickering light of myriad tiny lamps and deities studded with jewels held court under gem-spangled canopies. Even today, the coffers of many Indian temples overflow with extraordinary riches that defy description.

The Idol's Eye diamond was unearthed in the mines of Golconda probably around the

Edward VII, prior to his coronation, formally receiving the grand, bejewelled maharajas of India at a royal durbar.

beginning of the 17th century. This luscious stone, weighing 70.21 carats, possesses a blue tint that is typical of the finest Indian diamonds.

In 1607, the East India Company seized it from Rahab, a Persian prince, as a repayment for his debts. It seems to have acquired its name from a legend describing it as an eye of an idol in the Temple of Benghazi in the Ottoman Empire. According to a story, an Ottoman ruler had abducted Princess Rashida from her lover, the raja of Kashmir. The Idol's Eye, from the raja's treasury, was given as ransom for her safe return.

The East India Company crest.

Much later, it was offered for sale at Christie's in London on July 14, 1865, and was described in their catalogue as "a splendid large diamond known as the Idol's Eye set round with 18 smaller brilliants and frame-work of small brilliants". It was bought at the auction by an unknown buyer named 'B.B.'. It is believed that the gem later passed on to the 34th Ottoman sultan, Abdul Hamid II. A despotic ruler, he was eventually deposed in 1909 by the Young Turks, a group of opponents within his own people. Aware of the volatile political situation, he decided to send his jewels to a safe place for future use. Encasing them securely, he entrusted them to a servant but unfortunately for the sultan, the avaricious vassal sold these jewels in Paris. This is probably how the Idol's Eye came to be one of the many large diamonds in possession of the Parisian dealer, Solomon Habib, who put them up for auction in Paris on June 24, 1909.

Christie's, London, where the stone was auctioned in 1865.

After the Second World War, the Idol's Eye was bought by a Dutch dealer who sold it in 1946 to the renowned New York jeweller Harry Winston. In 1947, the year India was taking spectacular strides towards independence, the Idol's Eye was sold by Winston to May Bonfils Stanton, the daughter of Frederick G Bonfils, publisher of the *Denver Post*.

Known for her beauty, Stanton loved jewellery and she began collecting it from a very young age. She lived alone in her palatial home and it is reported that every morning when she sat down to a solitary breakfast, laid out on her monogrammed china, the Idol's Eye sparkled around her neck! She was in her eighties when she died in 1962, and Parke-Bernet Galleries Inc of New York auctioned her collection. The proceeds of the sale went to the various charities she had favoured.

The Idol's Eye was bought by the Chicago jeweller Harry Levinson for $375,000. In 1973, Levinson offered the diamond for a public sale but withdrew it when it failed to reach his minimum asking price of $1 million. In 1979, the London jeweller, Laurence Graff, bought the Idol's Eye. In January 1983, Graff sold the stunning gem along with the 41.94-carat Emperor Maximilian diamond and a 70.54-carat fancy yellow diamond, named after the Ottoman sultan, to a buyer who remained anonymous. The sale of the three stones to a single purchaser is thought to be one of the most expensive diamond transactions of all time.

Weight: 46.39 CARATS & 44.14 CARATS
Cut/Shape: BRILLIANT/PEAR
Colour: COLOURLESS
Owner: ROBERT MOUAWAD, PARIS

The maharajas of India led privileged lives, full of legendary splendour and unimaginable riches. Draped in brocade and silk, they wore ropes of pearls, ate off monogrammed gold and slept on perfumed silk sheets. Their days were spent preparing for the fabulous parties they hosted and each night their marbled palaces shimmered in the iridescence of Tiffany lamps, as huge silver salvers of food were offered to bejewelled guests. But this life of luxury and privilege was delicately balanced with voracious gossip, sinister plots and political intrigue.

The almost identical Indore Pears were once part of the collection of the Holkars, the maharajas of Indore.

Tukoji Rao III, the Maharaja of Indore, lived just such a luxurious, double-layered life. The story of the Indore Pears, the two pear-shaped Golconda gems that weighed 46.95 and 46.70 carats, and which he owned, is an expression of the flamboyant nature of his personal life.

One cool evening in January 1925, a car was making its way along the ridge of Malabar Hill, one of the most expensive residential areas of Bombay, towards the leafy Hanging Gardens. The occupants of the car were an official of the Bombay Corporation, a friend of his, and a woman. Suddenly, out of nowhere, another car appeared carrying assailants who attacked them, killing the official and injuring the others. Speculations about the possible murderers and their motives swept through the city; the Bombay police offered a reward of Rs 10,000 for any information about the crime.

When the case was put before the Bombay High Court, it was revealed that the woman had been a dancing girl in the court of the Maharaja of Indore. Her name was Mumtaz Begum and she had also been the maharaja's

View from Malabar Hill. Bombay.

The scene of the brutal murder which resulted in the Indore Pears leaving India.

courtesan. He was madly in love with her but she did not reciprocate his feelings and one day she escaped from the maharaja's entourage, hopping off his private train as it halted for a stop. She proceeded via Amritsar to Bombay where she became the ward of a rich merchant.

Mumtaz Begum identified the attackers as the maharaja's men who were members of the Indore police and infantry. Though his name was never disclosed, the maharaja was given the option of appearing at an official enquiry or abdicating in favour of his seventeen-year-old son, Yashwant Rao. He chose to abdicate and stormed off to Europe in a royal huff. While in Switzerland, he met Nancy Anne Miller, a rich young American from Seattle. They were married in 1928 and she became his third wife. The bride converted to Hinduism and changed her name to Sharmishtha Devi Holkar in anticipation of wedded bliss. The enamoured bridegroom showered his wife with expensive gifts, among which were the Indore Pears.

The honeymoon did not last long and the maharaja and his wife soon got divorced. After this parting, the Indore Pears were sold to Harry Winston. He had them recut to 46.39 and 44.14 carats, and displayed both diamonds in his exhibition, 'The Court of Jewels'. From 1953 to 1976, they crisscrossed paths between Winston and several clients including at least one royal person. The diamonds were eventually auctioned by Christie's, Geneva, in 1980, and again in 1987. Robert Mouawad is their present owner.

The two scintillating Indore Pear diamonds, exquisitely set in a pair of earrings.

SHAH
TO PLACATE THE TSAR

Weight: 88.70 CARATS
Cut/Shape: UNCUT/NARROW OBLONG
Colour: PALE YELLOW
Location: KREMLIN, MOSCOW

A glass model of the Shah diamond. The stone's colour, limpidity and the inscriptions on its three faces, make it one of the most precious relics in the world today.

The ownership of great gemstones had been the privilege of royalty from the beginning of time. Only kings and queens had the wealth to buy or the power to seize them. However, the rise of democracies led to the decline of monarchies and powerful financial tycoons replaced rulers as the buyers of expensive jewels. More and more of the collectors who frequented world auctions were wealthy commoners who could afford the fabulous prices. Then, another trend started emerging. Many celebrated diamonds passed from the august private collections of individuals to the public displays of world-famous museums. Today, these museums are willing to spend millions of dollars on a single stone. The Shah diamond is representative of this latter trend.

Only a few of the world's legendary gemstones have escaped being geometrically patterned by man. The Shah diamond, which is not cut, is a tangible symbol of centuries of vicissitudes. However, this Golconda gem has been polished in parts and reduced from its original weight of 95 carats to 88.70 carats. Pale yellow in colour, the irregularly-shaped Shah has three smooth cleavage faces while the fourth one is faceted and is representative of an early form of a Mughal style of cutting that prevailed in India. The diamond, which has never been set in a jewel for personal adornment, is superbly engraved on the three cleavage faces with the names of the three rulers who owned it. The stories unveiled through these inscriptions have made the Shah a diamond of perennial interest to historians and jewel lovers all over the world.

The first date on the stone is the year 1000 in the Muslim calendar (1591 in the English calendar), and the king mentioned along with this date is Bourhan Nizam Shah II, the ruler of Ahmadnagar. This kingdom, situated near Bijapur, was invaded by the Mughal emperor Shah Jahan in 1636.

A miniature painting depicting Emperor Aurangzeb at the siege of Golconda in 1687. The Mughal victory in this battle gave them access to the diamond mines in that region.

The next date on the diamond is 1051 (1641), and the delicate lettering reads, "Son of Jahangir Shah. Jahan Shah 1051". From this progression of dates it can be assumed that the ice-sheer Shah fell in the hands of the Mughal emperor when he took possession of Bourhan II's palace and wealth. Shah Jahan was succeeded by Aurangzeb, the third of his four sons, and the diamond passed on to him as a dynastic heirloom. In 1665, when Jean-Baptiste Tavernier went to Aurangzeb's palace to take leave of the emperor, he was shown into the ornate court and his description of what he saw is recorded in his reports: "On the side of the throne which is opposite the Court, there is to be seen a jewel consisting of a diamond of about 80 to 90 carats weight, with rubies and emeralds around it, and when the King is seated he has this jewel in full view." It is very likely that the beautiful Shah was similarly suspended, for on its upper part there is a fine groove that was possibly carved to hold the silken rope from which it hung.

The third name inscribed on the diamond is that of the Perisan ruler Sultan Qajar Fath Ali Shah, and the year is 1824. After the plunder of Delhi in 1739, Nadir Shah carried away to Persia an unimaginable quantity of riches, including the Shah

Nadir Shah, the Persian ruler who invaded Delhi in 1739 and carried away unimaginable treasures.

diamond, which stayed in that country for nearly a century, passing from one ruler to the next.

In 1827, a disagreement arose between Persia and Russia and war was declared involving the two nations. Persia was strong and its serried troops would have marched bravely towards victory, but Fath Ali Shah was frugal and refused to pay his soldiers during the cold winter. The unhappy troops made their way back home. In 1838, Russia won the war and coerced Persia into signing the Treaty of Turkmanchai under the leadership of Alexander Sergeyevich Griboyedoff.

Alexander Griboyedoff (above), the Russian diplomat, whose death at the hands of the Persians proved to be a milestone in the journey of the Shah diamond (below).

In recognition of his services during the war, Griboyedoff was appointed the Russian ambassador to Persia. However, the Persians disliked him and opposed him vociferously. Events came to a head when two girls of Russian-Armenian origin escaped from Ali Shah's harem and sought the help of their compatriots to return to their homeland. Griboyedoff offered them protection but this deed was to cost him his life. The Persians were so annoyed with his interference that they killed him.

The Shah diamond was presented to Tsar Nicholas I to avoid a war between Persia and Russia.

Fath Ali Shah, nervous and contrite, immediately sent the Russian ruler, Tsar Nicholas I, a gift in order to placate him and circumvent the chance of another battle. The present that made its way to St Petersburg was the Shah.

At the start of the First World War, in 1914, the diamond was taken from the Diamond Room in the White Palace at St Petersburg and transported to Moscow for safe keeping. Today, it is a part of the treasures in the Russian Diamond Fund and is on display at the Kremlin, which is its proud custodian. The pellucid Shah, with its meticulous lettering, is perhaps one of the most valuable museum pieces in existence.

Akbar Shah
THE LUSTRE OF THE PEACOCK THRONE

Weight: 73.60 CARATS
Cut/Shape: IRREGULAR/PEAR
Colour: COLOURLESS
Owner/Location: UNKNOWN

The rulers of the Mughal dynasty had a passion for chronicling their reign and almost every emperor in that lineage commissioned lavishly illustrated biographies. These documents have proved to be invaluable resources for later historians who have been able to use them to reconstruct social and political events during the lives and times of the Mughal emperors.

These meticulously recorded volumes have been especially valuable in reconstructing the story of the historic Akbar Shah diamond. This fabulous gem, which once weighed 116 carats, is said to have borne two inscriptions in Persian. One referred to its first owner, Emperor Jahangir. According to the etching, the stone found its way into the Imperial Treasury of the emperor in 1619. A possible allusion to this can be found in the *Tuzuk-i-Jahangiri* (*Memoirs of Jahangir*). These records, either written in Jahangir's own hand or dictated to a scribe, cover the period of his reign (1605-27) and illustrate his glamorous lifestyle. Of his sojourn in Gujarat, it is recorded: "On Friday the 5th Bahram, son of Jahangir Quli Khan, came from the province of Bihar, and had the good fortune to pay his respects. He laid before me some diamonds he had obtained from the mine at Kokhra."

The two inscriptions in Persian that were carved on the tantalising Akbar Shah diamond.

It is likely that the Akbar Shah was among the array of diamonds that were presented to Jahangir. It is interesting to note that the memoirs make a mention of diamond deposits "from the mine at Kokhra" (present day Khukra, 64 km west of Ranchi) in the eastern state of Bihar. Apparently, these were not from a mine at all, but from a river bed that was fertile with diamonds. Though Jahangir's memoirs give a detailed description of how large diamonds were also mined from this source, this area has rarely been given due credit by the diamond mining industry. In fact, it is hardly ever mentioned as a diamond rich region of India.

The second inscription on the Akbar Shah confirms that it officially became a part of Shah Jahan's treasury in 1629. It is widely believed by historians that this celebrated gem was set as one of the eyes of the peacock in the fabulous Peacock Throne. However, other scholars suggest the possibility of it being the dazzling diamond encircled by emeralds and rubies, suspended opposite the throne. But there are yet other authorities who feel that the suspended gem was the Shah diamond.

Shah Jahan ordered the construction of the Peacock Throne and it was created under the supervision of Bebadul Khan during the course of seven years. The throne sat resplendent in the Mughal court till 1739 when the Persian ruler Nadir Shah looted Delhi and seized the throne as part of his booty.

Much later, in 1866, the Akbar Shah was reported to be in Constantinople, where it had come to be known as the Shepherd's Stone. It was bought by George Blogg of the London firm of Blogg & Martin and was carried to London where it was recut to 73.60 carats. This

The crest of the royal Gaekwad family of Baroda.

cutting, however, turned out to be no better than a heart-rending act of vandalism; Levi Moses Auerhaan, the cutter of the extraordinary gem, had by an unforgivable mistake succeeded in completely grinding off the intricate inscriptions on the stone, leaving it a historical cripple. Nevertheless, the following year, Blogg succeeded in selling the glossy diamond to Mulhar Rao, the Gaekwad of Baroda, for £35,000.

A painting depicting the Mughal emperor Shah Jahan seated on the famous Peacock Throne, also known as Takht-e-Taous and now on display in Tehran along with the Iranian Crown Jewels.

It was common knowledge among jewellers the world over that the maharajas of India owned unrivalled collections of glittering jewels and they had the wealth to acquire more. From the time of the 1911 Delhi Durbar,

keen representatives from all the famous jewellery houses of Europe such as Cartier, Boucheron and Garrard, were known to travel to India, singularly intent on tempting the deliciously insouciant royals with specially crafted designs for their gems. Living it up in their host's pretty palaces, they vied with each other to gratify the royal fancy. By 1926, the new ruler of Baroda, Sayaji Rao Gaekwad III, had commissioned Jacques Cartier to reset his entire jewellery collection in platinum, beginning to be considered more fashionable than gold. The Akbar Shah, a part of the Baroda collection, was among the gems that were delicately styled in a cool, silvery setting.

That is the last known fact about the radiant Akbar Shah. One can only conjecture about its present whereabouts; perhaps it still nestles in the regal jewellery assemblage in Baroda.

George V at the 1911 Delhi Durbar where he was honoured as the King-Emperor (above) by the maharajas of India. A coin depicting Sayaji Rao Gaekwad III (right), once the owner of the Akbar Shah.

SHAH JAHAN TABLE-CUT
THE CLUE IN THE MUGHAL MINIATURE

Weight: 56.70 CARATS

Cut/Shape: TABLE/OCTAGON

Size: LENGTH 33.00 MM, WIDTH 46.00 MM, DEPTH 3.00 MM

Colour: PALE PINK

Owner: SHEIKH NASSER AL-SABAH, KUWAIT

Clear as a shard of ice, the Shah Jahan Table-Cut diamond is now part of a private jewellery collection in Kuwait.

The era of the Mughal emperors has always been evocative of extravagance, romance and exquisite artistry. Tales of fabulous jewels, handsome princes, beautiful women and perfumed palaces have created an aura of splendour that continues to linger long after the end of the dynasty in 1858. The Mughals were great patrons of the arts, and artists were respected and encouraged. Painters were often allowed to examine at close quarters priceless jewels and textiles belonging to the emperors, to reproduce in their paintings. One of these exquisite miniature paintings is especially significant in the story of the Shah Jahan Table-Cut diamond.

On May 16, 1985, Christie's offered for auction "a spectacular historic table-cut diamond" in Geneva. It was an unmounted gem weighing 56.70 carats, octagonal in shape with distinctly drilled holes. Before the sale, it was inspected by E A Jobbins and Dr R R Harding of the Institute of Geological Sciences. In the course of the examination, a remarkable connection was made between the diamond they were examining and a Mughal miniature painting dated 1616-17, displayed in the Victoria & Albert Museum. This painting is an image of the Mughal emperor Shah Jahan holding a *sarpech* (turban ornament or aigrette) in his left hand and pointing to it with his right. This beautiful jewel is made of gold and has mounted, within its arabesque border, a cushion-shaped apple green emerald and an octagonal table-cut diamond. From the crown of the emerald rises a spray of curved gold, each stem ending in a pearl droplet. The diamond in the jewelled ornament closely matched the stone that was being examined by the two gemmologists. This resemblance became even more apparent when Shah Jahan's hand holding the *sarpech* was enlarged. Both the dimensions and the shape of the gem in the painting matched

This miniature painting of Emperor Shah Jahan holding a turban ornament containing the Shah Jahan Table-Cut diamond helped confirm the gem's identity.

Edwin Streeter, the famous 19th-century authority on diamonds.

those of the table-cut diamond being studied. Unquestionably, this was the Shah Jahan Table-Cut.

A reference to the diamond can be found in the accounts of Jean-Baptiste Tavernier. After deposing Shah Jahan, his son Aurangzeb became the Mughal emperor in 1658. On November 2, 1665, Tavernier went to his court to pay his respects. On that occasion, Akel Khan, chief of the emperor's treasury, showed him some of the royal jewels. In addition to the Great Mughal, the collection included "another diamond of pear shape of very good form and fine water, with three other diamonds, table-shaped, two of them clean and the third with some little black specks. Each weighs fifty-five to sixty ratis, and the pear sixty-two and half."

Edwin Streeter, the 19th-century London jeweller and an authority on diamonds and gemstones, states in his book, *The Great Diamonds of the World*, that according to Tavernier's calculations, the weight of the three table-cut stones in Aurangzeb's treasury would have been from 48 to 52 (old) carats. Christie's sale catalogue makes a reference to this, taking as given that it is nearly impossible to verify the accuracy of Tavernier's assessment of the gems, made more than three centuries ago. Streeter has also suggested that in all probability the beautiful diamond was part of the booty taken away to Persia by the infamous Nadir Shah after the sack of Delhi in 1739.

In 1741, Nadir Shah sent his representative to Russia with several priceless gifts for the newly-proclaimed Empress Elizabeth. There were huge trays piled high with jewellery, and possibly, one of them carried the Shah Jahan Table-Cut diamond. It is probable that one of the tsars or tsarinas later presented it to someone.

More than a hundred years later, the gem resurfaced in London. In the astringent summer of 1851, the world's most celebrated and beautiful jewellery was displayed at the Great Exhibition that was held in Hyde Park. *The Times* reported the event stating that "In the British department, among the gorgeous and costly display of jewellery and gold and silver plate, there is a small case which attracts considerable attention. It contains imitations in crystal of all the largest diamonds in the world." One of these models was the Shah Jahan Table-Cut.

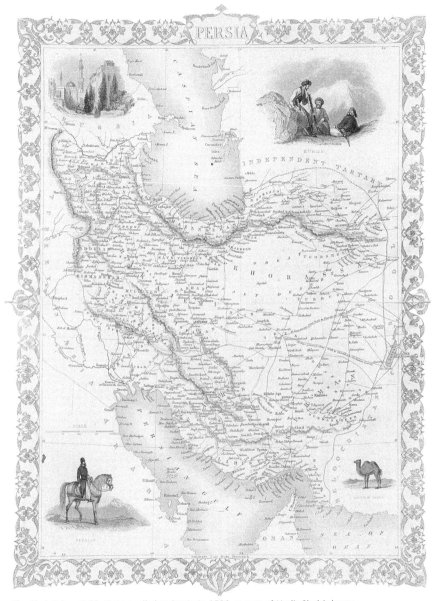

The Shah Jahan Table-Cut travelled to Persia in 1739 as part of Nadir Shah's booty.

At the 1985 Christie's sale, the Shah Jahan Table-Cut remained unsold and the vendor announced that it was acquired by his family in 1893. It was later sold privately and is now owned by Sheikh Nasser Al-Sabah of Kuwait.

ARCOTS

THE BRILLIANCE OF THE WESTMINSTER TIARA

Weight: ARCOT I – 30.99 CARATS; ARCOT II – 18.85 CARATS
Cut/Shape: BRILLIANT/PEAR
Colour: COLOURLESS
Owner/Location: ARCOT I – SHEIKH AHMED HASSAN
FITAIHI, SAUDI ARABIA; ARCOT II – UNKNOWN

"... fixed by themselves on the safety-pin they looked extremely bogus, so that a friend who saw me that evening remarked, 'What on earth does Loelia think she's doing, pinning those two lumps of glass on herself?'"
– Duchess of Westminster.
The Arcot I (above).

The imperial rulers of the British Raj seem to have mysteriously become the owners of countless Indian treasures – all recorded in their journals as a *nazrana*, a gift offered to a ruler as an expression of loyalty. Possibly, the gems presented by Azim-ud-Daula, the Nawab of Arcot, to Queen Charlotte, the consort of King George III of Great Britain, in 1777, were also a *nazrana*. The queen received several diamonds from the nawab, of which two were pear-shaped drops known as the Arcot diamonds, weighing 33.70 and 23.65 carats.

The Arcots, unearthed from the famous diamond mines in Golconda, were particularly well received by the queen whose passion for jewels was widely known. As they had been a personal gift, they were not considered a part of the crown jewels. Queen Charlotte instructed in her will that the diamonds be sold after her death and the proceeds be divided among her four daughters or their survivors who were to "share and share alike".

However, after her death in 1818, her last wishes were disregarded by her eldest son. Following his father's death in 1820, he appropriated the family property, money and all

Queen Charlotte (right) received the Arcots as a gift in 1777. The Nawab of Arcot (facing page) is said to have presented several jewels to the English royalty.

PLAYER'S CIGARETTES

CHARLOTTE OF MECKLENBURG

his mother's jewellery, ascended the throne as King George IV, and had the Arcot diamonds set in his crown.

When George IV died, John Bridge of Rundell & Bridge & Co, the crown jewellers, bought the Arcots. In 1831, they were mounted in a gorgeous crown made for Queen Adelaide, to wear at the coronation of her husband William IV, the successor of George IV. There was nothing unusual about this loan as it was customary for the royal family to borrow precious jewels from the crown jewellers for state occasions.

On July 20, 1837, the Arcots were offered for sale at an auction held at Willis's Rooms in London. They were bought by the first Marquess of Westminster, who also purchased the Nassak diamond, for £11,000 as a birthday present for his wife. Thereafter, the two dazzling drops were set in a variety of jewels for almost a century and in 1930, the second Marquess of Westminster had them set in a magnificent tiara designed by the Parisian jeweller Lacloche. The Westminster Tiara, fashioned to fit on the head like an upright hairband, was set with, apart from the Arcots, a round brilliant weighing 32.30 carats in the centre and 1,421 smaller diamonds. The beautiful ornament was made up of baguette, marquise and round diamonds set in *pavé*-style arches which encircled delicate diamond nibs, with the Arcots set amid a cluster of large round stones. The centrepiece could be detached and worn as a brooch and the Arcots were designed to double as earrings. The celebrated photographer, Cecil Beaton, photographed Duchess

The Westminster Tiara (above), into which the Arcots were set, was designed by the Parisian jeweller Lacloche. Loelia, the Duchess of Westminster, apparently wearing the Arcots in a brooch (facing page).

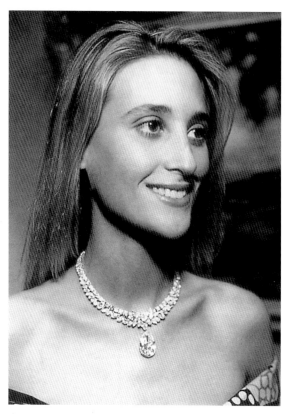

The daughter-in-law of Harry Winston, the famous New York jeweller, wearing the Arcot I in a necklace.

Loelia, the duke's third wife, wearing this tiara in 1931, and later his fourth wife was also often seen wearing it.

After the death of the second Marquess of Westminster, the tiara was auctioned by Sotheby's in London on June 25, 1959. It was bought by Harry Winston for £110,000, which was then a world record price for a piece of jewellery. He had the Arcots recut for greater brilliance to 30.99 carats and 18.85 carats. The stones were subsequently split up and sold as solitaire rings to two private clients. The larger diamond was referred to as Arcot I and the smaller one as Arcot II. The tiara, which was not broken up and could be worn without the removable diamonds, was sold, again by Sotheby's, to a client in Texas.

A more recent owner of Arcot I, known to be a lady of title, wore it as a pendant suspended from a ravishing necklace created by the jewellers, Van Cleef & Arpels, Paris. The bewitching stone and the necklace were offered for sale by her at an auction on November 17, 1993 by Christie's at Geneva. The expected price was 2 million Swiss francs (more than £800,000). At the event, both the Arcot and the necklace were sold to Sheikh Ahmed Hassan Fitaihi of Saudi Arabia for an amazing sum of £918,243.

The Arcot I suspended from a spectacular necklace. Harry Winston especially popularised this setting, inspired by a holly wreath, where the leaves themselves lend a circular shape. He applied the principle to gems and allowed them to shape the jewellery.

POLAR STAR
THE BRIGHTEST DIAMOND EVER SEEN

The Polar Star diamond, like its celestial counterpart, shines with a mystical beauty. Due to its perfect cut, an eight-point star is visible on its pavilion.

Weight: 41.28 CARATS
Cut/Shape: BRILLIANT/OBLONG CUSHION
Colour: TRACE OF ROSE
Owner/Location: UNKNOWN

Although little is known about the history of the Polar Star, it is important to include this gem in a compilation of famous Indian diamonds, if only for its singular beauty. It is arguably the best cut historic diamond ever, a cut so symmetrical that the stone can be balanced on its culet. It is easy to see a perfect eight-point star on its pavilion and this is from where the gem derives its name. Even today, this Golconda diamond remains the epitome of brilliance and celebrates man's creativity as a tangible, glittering star, a truly magical reflection of its distant celestial twin.

The Polar Star was first known to be owned by Joseph Bonaparte, elder brother of the French emperor Napoleon. An avid jewel collector, he acquired the gem from a mysterious source. After he lost his kingdom, comprising Naples and Spain, he sold it and sailed off to America.

The next recorded owner of the dazzling gem was Princess Tatiana Youssoupov, who lived from 1769 to 1841. She belonged to one of the richest and most important families in imperial Russia. During the family's ownership of the diamond, it also came to be known as the Youssoupov.

After the Russian Revolution broke out, Tatiana's brother, Prince Felix Youssoupov fled from Russia taking with him the Polar Star. In 1924, he first offered the diamond to Cartier, who kept it at their London branch for a short period. He then pawned it along with some other jewels to the London firm, T M Sutton. Later, the Polar Star was redeemed by Cartier.

In 1928, Cartier sold the diamond to Lady Lydia Deterding, the wife of Sir Henry Deterding, founder of Royal Dutch Shell. Lady Deterding wished to have the Polar Star sold after her death and Christie's was authorised by the executers of her will to do so. The auction took place on November 20, 1980 in Geneva and the Polar Star was knocked down to an anonymous Sri Lankan dealer for 8 million Swiss francs. It is probably still in Sri Lanka.

Prince Felix Youssoupov took the Polar Star with him when he left Russia. He later offered it to Cartier.

TERESCHENKO
A WORLD-RECORD PRICE

Weight: 42.92 CARATS
Cut/Shape: BRILLIANT/PEAR
Colour: BLUE
Owner: ROBERT MOUAWAD, PARIS

Many of the world's ancient diamonds seem to have suddenly resurfaced from the dark waters of anonymity during the last century. Their earlier owners, journeys and adventures are mysteriously unknown; they either go unrecorded or are so nebulous as to have no relevance in their study. Over the years, a few of these old gems have become so steeped in myth and legend that sorting out fact from fantasy would take many years for even the most diligent researcher.

The Tereschenko is one such diamond whose story surfaces as late as the 20th century. While it is known that this pear-shaped fancy blue stone was unearthed in the Kollur alluvial deposits in Golconda, how it made its journey to Russia remains a mystery. The diamond's first recorded owners were the Tereschenko family, the sugar barons of Russia. In 1915, Mikhail Tereschenko, who later became the minister of foreign affairs, asked the jeweller Jacques Cartier to set the stone as the centrepiece in a necklace made with an assortment of fancy-coloured diamonds. Like juicy, crystallised fruit, their colours were described by Cartier as "jonquil, lemon, aquamarine, sultana-green, gold button, grey, blue, crevet, lilac, rose, old port, madeira and topaz". Without doubt, the beautiful necklace was a masterpiece of shimmering colours. In 1917, just before the Russian Revolution, the Tereschenko was in all probability dislodged from the necklace, smuggled out of Russia by its owners, and sold to a private buyer.

The gem spent nearly seven decades in sequestered splendour, coming into public view only in 1984, when Christie's declared that they would be auctioning the fourth largest recorded fancy blue diamond. On November 14, 1984 at 10 pm, amid the animated buzz of buyers at Hotel Richmond, Christie's chairman announced the start of the bidding at 3 million Swiss francs. Forty seconds later, the bidding reached 6.5 million, far beyond the price expected by even the most experienced auctioneers. The Tereschenko was finally knocked down to Robert Mouawad, who paid 10 million Swiss francs (£3,180,000) for it, a record price for a diamond.

A diamond is forever; whatever its price today, a better one is guaranteed tomorrow. At 142 carats to an ounce it represents the most compact and

Jacques Cartier set this beautiful stone with a cascade of fruit-coloured gems in a necklace ordered by the Russian sugar baron, Mikhail Tereschenko, in 1915.

portable of investments because a beautiful diamond weighing even half as much can easily fetch millions of dollars. It is understandable why no one is ever surprised by exorbitant diamond prices. The electrifying race to acquire them continues.

QUEEN OF HOLLAND
A CRICKETER'S DELIGHT

Weight: 135.92 CARATS
Cut/Shape: BRILLIANT/CUSHION
Colour: BLUE TINT
Owner: ROBERT MOUAWAD, PARIS

The year 1886 was the first time an Indian cricket team played in England. A boy of fourteen, who was to become one of the beacons of the game in that country and in the world of cricket, was at the time busy practicing his cover-drive in the princely state of Nawanagar in Kathiawar. Ranjitsingh, affectionately known as 'Ranji', was to later become the Maharaja of

"There was talk of the Jam Saheb's seventy two centuries in first-class cricket, 'supple, dusky legerdemain'; and of how a strange light out of the East was seen on English fields when he batted."
– Ann Morrow in Highness.

Nawanagar. He went to Cambridge University in 1892 and after completing his studies proceeded to pursue what he loved best – cricket. He played for England, captained Sussex from 1899 to 1903, and soon came to be known as the 'Prince of Cricket', cutting a glamorous, charismatic figure as he stood at the wicket, his silk shirt fluttering gracefully in the cool English breeze. By 1897, he had already ranked fifth in the national averages and it seemed that he could never have a disappointing season; between 1895 and 1904 his annual score exceeded a thousand runs.

Ranjitsingh became Maharaja of Nawanagar in 1906. A modern and cultured ruler, he was very fond of jewels. The Nawanagar emerald collection was unparalleled in the world and Cartier is said to have added to it a necklace of 17 rectangular emeralds including a 70-carat gem, which once belonged to a Turkish sultan, two turban ornaments with a 56-carat and a 39-carat emerald, and a two-string emerald-bead necklace.

The Queen of Holland diamond first caught Ranjitsingh's fancy in 1930. Named after Holland's Queen Wilhelmina, this 136.25-carat gem was then owned by the Dutch jewellery firm, F Friedman & Co, who had also cut it. This lovely stone was discovered at Golconda and although it was white and flawless, the Gemological Institute of America later designated it as 'intense blue' because of its blue tint. It is the second largest diamond to be classified by the institute as D-flawless, the highest grade in colour and clarity, to date, the largest one being the South African Premier Rose, weighing 137.02 carats.

An avid collector of jewels, Ranjitsingh was once the proud owner of the Queen of Holland diamond.

While in London, Ranjitsingh had his court jeweller contact Albert Monnickendam, an authority on diamonds. Monnickendam was invited to the maharaja's opulent home at Staines, just outside London. After a pleasant lunch, Ranjitsingh led him into a large room suffused with crisp, afternoon light and asked his servant to fetch him his jewel box. The big gold box was brought in and Ranjitsingh opened it, revealing the dazzling stone set in a pendant. He wanted Monnickendam's opinion on the diamond before purchasing it. Perfect in every way, Monnickendam certified it as one of the most beautiful diamonds in the world. Ranjitsingh then told his guest that the gem had once been part of the crown jewels of Russia.

Ranjitsingh eventually bought the Queen of Holland and had it set in a splendid necklace. Jacques Cartier, who created the necklace, was awestruck by the breathtaking diamond and referred to it as "a really superb realization of a connoisseur's dream".

In 1933, Ranjitsingh died, and in 1960, Cartier's London branch put the diamond up for sale, having bought it from the royal family. It was then purchased in 1978 by William Goldberg of New York who had it recut from its earlier weight of 136.25 carats to 135.92 carats, and soon sold it to another buyer for about $7 million. It now belongs to Robert Mouawad.

Thus, the Queen of Holland left the shores of India as quietly as it had entered. Ranjitsingh, its celebrated erstwhile owner, is known to millions as one of the most magical cricketers the world has ever produced, but perhaps only few people know of his great penchant for jewels and his particular fascination with the ravishing Queen of Holland diamond.

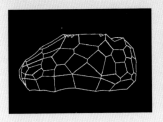  

BRIEF HISTORIES

Its color is that of ice,
and as the dew-drop or drop of water
from a mountain stream
sparkles in the light of the sun,
as the icicle sparkles in winter,
and the stars on a cold winter night,
so the diamond sparkles, and it combines
and contrasts with all known gems.

GEORGE FREDERICK KUNZ

ARCHDUKE JOSEPH

Little is known about the Archduke Joseph, a diamond named after the man who was, for a short time after 1918, the regent of Hungary. This was Joseph August Clemence Maria, Archduke of Austria and Palatinate of Hungary, who belonged to the great dynastic House of Habsburg. At the end of the Second World War, when Soviet troops occupied Hungary, he emigrated to the United States of America. He gave the diamond to his son, Joseph Francis, who on June 1, 1933, was stated to have left it in the Hungarian General Credit Bank, in the presence of a state counsellor and a few officials from the National Bank of Hungary. How this diamond, unearthed in the Golconda mines in India, came to be in the possession of a Hungarian ruler is a mystery.

The Archduke Joseph diamond is softly luminous, which greatly enhances its beauty and value.

Weighing 78.54 carats, the Archduke Joseph has an elongated cushion shape and a mixed cut. The stone possesses a pure, beautiful colour and a luminosity that is typical of the finest Indian diamonds. According to the New York jeweller, Harry Winston, there is a slight flaw in the Archduke Joseph, manifest in a white line. In 1936, this fabulous gem was sold to an anonymous buyer and it was kept in a secret place until 1961.

On June 22, 1961, when this marvellous diamond came up for sale in London at Sotheby's, it was thought to be the largest loose gem of such a high standard ever to be auctioned in Great Britain. In spite of the usual excitement which accompanies every important diamond sale, the bidding for the Archduke Joseph during this auction halted rather prematurely at £145,000. The gem was withdrawn from the sale as it had fared so poorly and had in all probability not even attracted its reserve price.

Later, it was reported that a consortium of jewellers from Hatton Garden, London's famous diamond quarter, had made an offer of purchase for the Archduke Joseph, which was rejected. This exquisite diamond then came up for auction in November 1993 when it was sold by Christie's for $6,487,945 to a private buyer. The diamond is believed to have since been resold to another collector.

The diamond set in a glorious necklace designed by Van Cleef & Arpels.

PRINCIE

A glass model of the Princie.

The Maharaja of Baroda, Pratapsingh Gaekwad, and his second wife, the beautiful Sita Devi, were a golden couple. They threw superb parties, whizzed off to Europe and America at a moment's notice and owned chests full of dazzling jewels. Their idyllic life lasted till 1956, the year they were divorced. The maharani went to France with their only child, the ten-year-old Prince Sayaji Rao Prataprao Gaekwad who was nicknamed 'Princie'. A compulsive spendthrift, she slipped gracefully into the Parisian high life; champagne parties, furs and film stars were all part of a day that began at two o'clock in the afternoon and ended at dawn. She took Paris by storm and her ruby-encrusted cigarette holder became her trademark. Princie was thoroughly indulged by his mother, and every evening the white Rolls-Royce, bearing the Baroda crest, would whisk mother and son off to a lively party.

One evening, the wilful maharani and the pampered prince breezed into the Paris branch of the jewellers, Van Cleef & Arpels, for a christening party. A beautiful cushion-shaped rose pink diamond, weighing 34.64 carats, was to be named. The little Gaekwad enchanted his hosts so much that they called the gem Princie after him.

The Princie diamond had been bought by Van Cleef & Arpels at a Sotheby's auction in London on March 17, 1960 for £46,000. The vendor had chosen to remain anonymous. At the time of the sale, the diamond was rumoured to have come from the Nizam of Hyderabad's magnificent collection of jewels, but some reports claimed that it had been a part of the state jewels of Turkey.

After the christening, Van Cleef & Arpels mounted the Princie diamond as a pendant on a necklace of baguette-cut diamonds, and sold it to an unknown buyer.

Jacques Arpels of the famous jewellery firm Van Cleef & Arpels, sitting on the left of the Maharaja of Baroda (above). Sita Devi (facing page), Maharani of Baroda, with her son Sayaji Rao Prataprao Gaekwad, who was nicknamed 'Princie'. The beautiful rose pink diamond was named after him.

AGRA

The exceptional purity and the rose pink colour of the Agra diamond, named after the historic city of Agra, is evocative of the regal splendour of the bygone Mughal era. From the time of its discovery, this diamond has been a much sought-after gem.

The Agra is believed to have belonged to the Mughal emperor Babur who acquired it, along with the Koh-i-Noor, from Raja Bikramajit of Gwalior after the Battle of Panipat in 1526. Babur is said to have worn this ravishing gem, which then weighed 41 carats, as an ornament in his turban.

One of its later owners is reported to be the Duke of Brunswick, an avid collector of diamonds in the 19th century. According to the catalogue of his diamond collection, he bought the gem in 1844 from the London diamond merchants Blogg & Martin.

The stone was later recut to remove some black spotty inclusions and its new weight was recorded as 32.24 carats. Around 1891, it became part of Edwin Streeter's collection. A great connoisseur of diamonds, Streeter sold his jewellery business to the Parisian jewellery firm, La Cloche Frères in 1904. The next year, his collection was sold by his successors through Christie's.

A view of the city of Agra, after which the diamond was named.

On February 22, 1905, Christie's auctioned the Agra. The room was packed with jewel lovers, including several Indian collectors. The bidding started at 1,000 guineas and the diamond was finally sold for 5,100 guineas to Max Meyer of Hatton Garden.

The Agra again came up for sale in 1909, this time in the collection of the dealer Salomon Habib. Soon after, the diamond was bought by Louis Winans through a firm of jewellers called Lewis & Sons. Winans had inherited a considerable fortune from his father, William Walter Winans, who had been a railroad engineer in Russia during the reign of Tsar Nicholas I. He had a considerable collection of spectacular diamonds and apart from the Agra, he possessed the Golden Drop, a pure yellow diamond.

In 1990, the heir to Louis Winans' estate offered the Agra for sale through Christie's. It was bought by SIBA Corporation of Hong Kong for £4,070,000 and has since been recut to 28.15 carats.

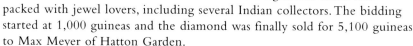

The Agra diamond is believed to have decorated the turban of Emperor Babur on several occasions.

DRESDEN GREEN

The pear-shaped Dresden Green diamond is unique due to its exceptional transparency and rare green colour.

This celebrated leaf green diamond is as luminous and clear as a forest drenched with prismatic raindrops. Cut into a modified pear-shaped brilliant with 58 facets, the Dresden Green weighs 40.70 carats and measures 29.75 mm long, 19.88 mm wide and 10.29 mm deep. The green colour, which is rare, is probably a result of the diamond's coming into contact with a radioactive substance at one point in its lifetime.

The history of the breathtakingly beautiful Dresden Green, which derives its name from the capital of Saxony, is surprisingly straightforward. The diamond was purchased by Frederick Augustus II, the Elector of Saxony, in 1741. He bought this gem, which had mysteriously made its way from the diamond mines of Golconda to the West, from a Dutch dealer named Delles at the Leipzig Fair.

The diamond became part of the crown jewels of Saxony and was set in a brooch called the Decoration of the Golden Fleece designed by the court jeweller Dinglinger. In 1746, this setting was broken up and the Elector ordered the Viennese jeweller, Pallard, to design another Golden Fleece, incorporating both the Dresden Green as well as the Dresden White, a 49.71-carat diamond. Twenty-two years later, another jeweller, Diessbach, set the Dresden Green in a hat clasp with two other white brilliants – together weighing almost 40 carats – and several smaller diamonds.

The crown jewels were on public display in Dresden Castle till the Second World War and in 1942 they were relocated to the Saxon Castle Königstein on the river Elbe. This move proved to be fortuitous; on February 13, 1945, Dresden was demolished by the sweeping air raids of the Allies. The castle which housed the jewels was totally destroyed.

Later that year, the Soviet Trophy Organisation took the crown jewels into its possession and had them sent to Moscow. In 1958, the Soviet government returned them to Germany where the glossy Dresden Green diamond is on display to this day in the rooms of the Green Vault, in the Albertinium Museum, Dresden.

The apple green colour and glossy fire of the Dresden Green is pure fantasy made real. Here, it is set in a sumptuous hat clasp that was designed by the jeweller Diessbach in 1768.

Nizam

Drawing of the Nizam diamond by geologist Henry Piddington.

The sixth Nizam of Hyderabad, Mahboob Ali Pasha, who acceded to the royal seat in 1911, was reputed to be one of the wealthiest men in the world. It is said that he had jewels worth £400 million, about £100 million in gold and silver, an annual income of £2 million, and 11,000 servants. His marbled palaces held treasures in jade and crystal, and his collection of pearls defied description.

The Nizams of Hyderabad had a penchant for jewels and it is only logical that a diamond found in the Golconda mines, which lay in the princely state of Hyderabad, should be called the Nizam. Interestingly, this gem was earlier known as Bala (little) Koh-i-Noor. Some accounts claim that Chandu Lal, the trusted minister of the fourth Nizam, Nasir-ud-Daula, acquired the diamond for him around 1835. It was safely kept in the Nizam's treasury, except during the period when it was mortgaged to raise funds to replenish the state finances. At this time, a glass replica was made to serve as a record. The gem was estimated to weigh 277 carats and was a partially cut stone of the finest water, possessing the colour and clarity of a true Golconda diamond. In 1891, the stone was inspected by a reporter from *San Francisco Chronicle* who compared its size to that of a champagne glass and estimated its value at £800,000, an unimaginable sum in those days! Today, the whereabouts of the Nizam diamond are unknown, although rumours of its sale or of it being the property of a royal Indian family continue to surface from time to time.

Chow Mahalla Palace (above), one of Mahboob Ali Pasha's (above right) many residences in Hyderabad.

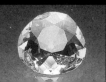

FOREIGN CONNECTIONS

While several famous diamonds were discovered in the mines of India, the country also played host to many well-known diamonds that travelled from distant shores. The tales of some of these magnificent stones are revealed here.

STAR OF THE SOUTH

In 1853, a black female slave working in the diamond deposits in Brazil found a stone weighing 254 carats. About the prevailing custom in these diamond mines, Edwin Streeter wrote: "If a negro finds one [diamond] from eight to ten carats weight, he receives two new shirts, a suit of clothes, a hat and a handsome knife." In this case, considering the size of the stone, the slave was rewarded with her freedom and a pension for life.

The slave's master, Casimiro de Tal, did not realise the real value of this amazing stone and he sold it to a shrewd buyer for a small sum of £3,000. The new owner promptly kept the diamond as collateral in the Bank of Rio de Janeiro and secured a hefty loan of £30,000.

Laxmi Vilas Palace, Baroda.

After passing through several hands, the diamond eventually arrived in Amsterdam to be cut. This task was entrusted to Voorzanger, of the reputed firm of Coster, who had earlier cut the Koh-i-Noor diamond. The result was a dazzling oval-shaped gem weighing 128.80 carats and measuring 35 mm long, 29 mm wide, and 19 mm deep.

Shortly after the diamond was cut, it was bought by a consortium of dealers in Paris. The chief of the consortium had it sent to India for a possible sale to an unidentified maharaja, but this transaction did not materialise. While still in India, stories about the diamond's beauty and purity reached the ears of Mulhar Rao Gaekwad, the ruler of Baroda, who was a passionate collector of jewels. He is said to have paid £80,000 for the gem.

The diamond was brought with great pomp and style to Laxmi Vilas, the Gaekwad's pistachio-and-gold marbled palace, famous for being three times the size of Buckingham Palace. Legend has it that owing to its great beauty and special value, the gem was placed on a saddled, caparisoned giraffe and ceremonially taken through the sun-dusted streets of Baroda till it eventually reached the palace. The Star of the South, along with another famous diamond known as the English Dresden, was set in a necklace of pear- and teardrop-shaped diamonds, which has adorned countless princesses of Baroda's royal family.

It is rumoured that the Star of the South diamond was subsequently sold to Rustomjee Jamsetjee of Bombay, and it is presumed that it may still be in the possession of his family.

JACOB

The Jacob diamond, also known as the Imperial, Great White or Victoria, was discovered in the Orange Free State in South Africa. It has never been clear whether it was unearthed in the Jagersfontein Mine, the Kimberley Mine or on the farm of a Dutchman who, for fear of attracting a mad rush of diamond hunters, kept it in a secret hiding place for a year before revealing its existence. However, the most widely believed version of its discovery relates how an officer of the Central Mining Company found a diamond weighing 457.50 (old) carats in the Kimberley Mine in 1884. He carried the stone out of the mine on his person and sold it illegally to a group of four diamond buyers. The magnificent gem then reached Cape Colony from where, after again being the focus of an illicit transaction, it sailed to London.

When it appeared in London, it caused a sensation in Hatton Garden, the diamond quarter of the city. The hunt for an eligible rich buyer soon commenced, but when none were forthcoming, a syndicate of eight persons, headed by a former resident of the Cape mines, bought the gem for £45,000. The syndicate decided to have the diamond cut and it was sent to the reputed Dutch firm of Jacques Metz. On April 9, 1887, in the presence of the Queen of Holland, the master cutter M B Barends began the fine faceting of the stone.

The Jacob diamond.

The process took a year and the result was a slightly oval-shaped brilliant with 58 facets, weighing 184.50 carats and measuring 39.50 mm long, 29.25 mm wide, and 22.50 mm deep.

The fabulous diamond was offered for sale and it joined one of the most enviable collections of jewellery when it came to be owned by the sixth Nizam of Hyderabad, Mahboob Ali Pasha. Reputedly the richest man in the world during the time, the Nizam's penchant for marvellous *objets d'art* had his Chow Mahalla Palace teeming with priceless treasures. The story of how he came to acquire the Jacob diamond is a fascinating one.

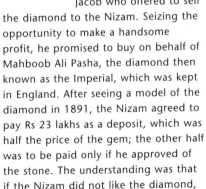

In 1871, a man by the name of Alexander Malcolm Jacob arrived in Simla and set himself up as a gem dealer. Jacob was variously supposed to be an Armenian, a Jew, and even a Russian or British agent. A bizarre character said to possess magical powers, it was Jacob who offered to sell the diamond to the Nizam. Seizing the opportunity to make a handsome profit, he promised to buy on behalf of Mahboob Ali Pasha, the diamond then known as the Imperial, which was kept in England. After seeing a model of the diamond in 1891, the Nizam agreed to pay Rs 23 lakhs as a deposit, which was half the price of the gem; the other half was to be paid only if he approved of the stone. The understanding was that if the Nizam did not like the diamond, the deposit would be returned to him. However, before the matter could proceed further, the British Resident at Hyderabad, Sir Denis Fitzpatrick, heard about the transaction and intervened in order to save the Nizam's government from bankruptcy. Later, when Alexander Jacob arrived in Hyderabad with the diamond, the Nizam expressed his dissatisfaction with the stone and refused to buy it. He demanded that the deposit be returned and as Jacob was unable to pay him back, the Nizam filed a case against him in the Calcutta High Court. Jacob was finally acquitted, however, the issue regarding the ownership of the diamond was settled out of court and the diamond was acquired by the Nizam for only half its asking price. Jacob did not receive the original price of the diamond that he had quoted to the Nizam and he was recompensed only for the legal costs. The case proved to be the cause of Jacob's bankruptcy and ruin. The Nizam, not particularly

Mir Osman Ali Khan, Nizam VII.

disturbed by the turn of events, simply wrapped up the diamond in an old ink-stained cloth and tossed it into a drawer. It is rumoured that the next Nizam, Mir Osman Ali Khan, eventually found it embedded in an old slipper that belonged to his father. He had the stone mounted on a gold filigree base and used it as a paperweight.

In 1948, after the integration of the princely states into the Union of India, questions relating to wealth, property, succession and inheritance of the former rulers became very important. In order to safeguard his wealth, Osman Ali Khan set up 'H.E.H. The Nizam's Jewellery Trust' in 1951. The Jacob diamond, which was assigned to this trust, was acquired by the government of India in 1995, along with the other jewels that formed a part of this trust. This impressive diamond was displayed for the first time in 2001 at the National Museum in New Delhi.

PORTER RHODES

The Porter Rhodes diamond, a beautiful octahedron weighing 153.50 carats, was unearthed in the Kimberley Mine in South Africa on February 12, 1880. This famous mine belonged to Porter Rhodes, who later went on to become one of the first directors of De Beers Consolidated Mines.

Porter Rhodes brought the gem to England and on January 19, 1881, he had an audience with the jewel-loving Queen Victoria to whom he showed this treasure. The queen was astounded by the sheer beauty and clarity of the stone. It was also shown to Empress Eugénie of France who was doubtful whether it had really come from South Africa, the diamonds from the country having earned a reputation of being yellowish in colour and therefore not very valuable. The brilliant white Porter Rhodes diamond helped in shattering this myth.

The stone was later cut and sold to the Baring-Gould family. In 1930, it was bought by the second Marquess of Westminster for his third wife, Duchess Loelia. It subsequently came to be owned by the London jewellers Jerwood & Ward, who sent it to Amsterdam where it was given its emerald cut. The diamond now weighed 56.60 carats.

A subsequent owner of the diamond was Maharaja Yashwant Rao of Indore, who bought it in 1937. He possessed fabulous treasures among which was his famous gold walking stick, encrusted with precious gems, and with a handle carved out of a single ruby. He was also the proud owner of four Jonker diamonds (V, VII, XI and XII) fashioned out of the 726-carat Jonker discovered in South Africa in 1934. Jonker I, reputed to be the most perfectly cut diamond in existence, and weighing 125.65 carats, is said to have once belonged to Queen Ratna of Nepal.

The Porter Rhodes diamond was bought by Harry Winston, the New York jewellery mogul, in 1946. He eventually sold it to a private client in Texas. This person in turn sold the gem through Sotheby's in October 1987. As autumn mists swirled around scarlet and copper trees, eager collectors made their way through the metallic mosaic of New York to the auction rooms of Sotheby's, where the celebrated diamond was eventually sold for $3.8 million to Laurence Graff, the London jeweller.

DE BEERS

In 1889, a stunning 439.86-carat diamond was unearthed in the De Beers Mine at Kimberley in South Africa. The enormous octahedron, pale lemon gold in colour, measured 47.60 mm at the longest axis. In all probability it was cut at Amsterdam as it was the premier diamond cutting centre at that time. The result was a cushion-shaped diamond weighing 234.50 carats, the stone having lost 205.36 carats in the process of cutting. Its impressive weight makes it the fourth largest polished diamond in the world, after Cullinan I, Cullinan II, and the Jubilee.

The De Beers was displayed at the Paris Exhibition in 1889. Soon after, it caught the eye of the imposing, six-feet tall, Maharaja of Patiala, Rajendra Singh, who bought the gem. A great lover of jewels, he could often be seen wearing waist-length ropes of pearls and emeralds, a belt of dazzling diamonds, a cluster of emeralds in his coal black turban and a four-inch emerald on a gold scarf, all at the same time. He favoured Savile Row suits, which he wore with pearl earrings as big as apricots. In fact, it is believed that Cartier at one time "filled casket after casket" of jewels for the maharaja. He had the striking De Beers diamond set as the centrepiece in a ceremonial necklace fashioned by Cartier.

The De Beers was sold in the 1930s to its present owners, who remain anonymous. They tried to sell the gem on May 6, 1982, in the auction rooms of Sotheby's, Geneva. There was a great deal of excitement as the bidding was expected to go up to $4.5 million. However, the radiant diamond failed to reach the undisclosed reserve price and has not resurfaced since then.

MAHJAL

In 1983, Christie's, Geneva, auctioned 'The Maharajah of Kapurthala Mahjal Diamond' for 1.32 million Swiss francs. This cushion-shaped gem, which possessed a deep golden colour, weighed 139.38 carats and was stated to be from South Africa.

The Mahjal diamond.

was made of 3,000 diamonds and pearls. He wore these clips in the pleats of his turbans that changed colour according to the season – yellow was meant for spring, rose pink for summer, and red was reserved for weddings.

It had once belonged to Jagatjit Singh, who was the Maharaja of Kapurthala from 1872 to 1949.

Jagatjit Singh had a flamboyant personality and was a devoted Francophile. He spoke excellent French, built a palace modelled on Versailles, employed French servants to look after his expensive French furniture and flew in renowned chefs from the Ritz hotel in Paris to serve exquisite French delicacies.

He also had a passion for jewels. It is said that he possessed a large number of turban clips, one of which

Maharaja Jagatjit Singh of Kapurthala.

The Mahjal was one of the many beautiful gems that adorned his colourful person and one can be certain that it was the perfect companion for the maharaja's beloved golden topaz, reputed to be one of the biggest in the world.

The name of the buyer at the 1983 Christie's auction has not been disclosed, and it is assumed that the Mahjal diamond still belongs to the same owner. In 1984, the stone was recut to 133.03 carats and its name was changed to Algeiba Star.

ENGLISH DRESDEN

The English Dresden, 119.50 carats in the rough, was discovered in 1857 in Brazil, and like many famous diamonds, it eventually made its way to India.

This stone was named after the London merchant, Edward Z Dresden. Dresden's agents bought the diamond in Rio de Janeiro on his behalf and dispatched it to London, from where the gem was sent for cutting to Coster in Amsterdam. This absolutely colourless and flawless stone, which was cut down to 78.53 carats, was fashioned into a finely proportioned pear shape.

Cotton merchants in the mid-1800s, Bombay.

The resulting stone was so pure that Dresden wrote in an account that it was the best diamond in the world. He had it matched against the Koh-i-Noor at the jewellers, Garrard, who said that the latter's colour had seemed yellowish in comparison to Dresden's diamond drop, which had been perfectly white.

Most people who saw the gem were fascinated by its water (transparency) and beauty, yet when offered for sale to various members of the European royalty, it was refused and it remained unsold for quite a while. The English Dresden then captured the interest of an unidentified maharaja, who went to London in 1863 with the singular intent of acquiring the bewitching gem. However, he did not agree to the asking price of £40,000 and had to return home disappointed. He had been accompanied by an English cotton merchant from Bombay who fell in love with the diamond and resolved to buy it. He found an opportunity to raise the required funds when, owing to a civil war in the United States of America, the price of cotton rose sharply.

The English merchant appointed an agent who offered Dresden £32,000 on his behalf. However, the agent slyly pocketed £8,000 in the bargain and informed his client from Bombay that Dresden's asking price had been £40,000. The deal completed, the English Dresden made its journey to India but soon after its arrival in Bombay, the merchant suddenly suffered heavy losses in his cotton business. One tragedy followed another and the merchant died leaving large debts which had to be paid off through the sale of the diamond. It was only logical that the enchanting gem be offered to Mulhar Rao Gaekwad of Baroda who was a keen collector of jewellery. He bought the diamond for £40,000.

The Gaekwad had the English Dresden set in a necklace along with the magnificent Star of the South, and it remained in the opulent Laxmi Vilas Palace in Baroda till 1934. It was later believed to have been sold to Cursetji Fardoonji, another collector from India, and is considered to be still in his family's possession.

THE GOLCONDA MINES

Marco Polo was one of the earliest Western travellers to relate stories about the fabulous wealth of India. He journeyed through the country in 1292 and wrote fascinating accounts of how large diamonds were discovered in riverbeds and on mountainsides that were watered by abundant rains. As he had not actually seen the diamond mines, his stories were rife with myths of sinister snakes and vicious eagles who were the guardians of these gems.

Myths apart, India was at that time beginning to be known as the treasury of diamonds. Gems of great size and value had been found over a vast area on the eastern side of the Deccan Plateau. This region lay in the territory of Golconda, which today covers the area that forms the state of Andhra Pradesh. It was here that India's most fabled and largest diamonds were unearthed. The Golconda mines, contrary to popular belief, were not confined to a small area around Golconda Fort. In fact, the entire region was rich with diamonds, and a bazaar trading in them flourished in the lanes around the fort. This ancient fort town lay five miles east of Hyderabad between the Godavari and Krishna rivers. It was chiefly in the alluvial deposits of the river Krishna that large diamonds were found.

One of the records about diamond mining in Golconda was left by a Portuguese physician, Garcia da Horta, who visited this region in 1565. He claimed that diamonds were extracted from rocks which were then allowed to 'rest' so as to facilitate new diamonds to form within them. This was obviously before people discovered that diamonds exist deep within the earth and that there are no diamond-producing rocks!

Between the 16th and the mid-19th centuries, there were nearly thirty mines in operation in Golconda. Prime amongst these was Kollur, located approximately 80 km from the Bay of Bengal, around the town of Elluru. Other well-known mines included Partiyala (situated close to Kollur), Gollapally, Mallavally, Ramallakota and Banganapally. Each of these mines were different; some were tunnels, others were open or deep pits. Jean-Baptiste Tavernier, the 17th-century French gem merchant, left records stating that the mines were discovered around 1445. According to his accounts, thousands of men crept along a roughly hewn, narrow passage deep under the ground to reach a large chamber. Here, the heat and lack of air were suffocating, so the workers went about their task naked. They searched especially for the colour of steel hidden in the buff-coloured clay. Much later in 1821, geologist H W Voysey visited the mines at Banganapally and wrote that they were made of materials, including a mixture of red and yellow jasper, that bore diamonds.

An earlier visitor, Henry Howard, had been to Golconda in the 1670s, and he wrote that diamonds were not found in clusters but in the veins of the earth, and were scattered over a large area. He also recorded the mining methods prevalent in the Golconda mines at that time. The pits were only a few feet deep and the soil that was dug up was relayed manually in open trays along a long line of workers. These workers were skilled enough to ascertain the existence of diamonds in a particular area and digging continued as per their judgement. When these precious gems, which were found embedded in round stones, were unearthed, they were brought up to the surface and kept in separate cisterns. Then they were washed with water, dried, and examined by the miners in

Diamonds being washed in the Ramallakota Mine.

bright sunlight in order to pick out those that were clear and sparkling. All the workers were Telugu-speaking natives and included women, and children as young as twelve years. There were 30,000 to 60,000 workers at every mine and each of them was constantly shifted to other mines to avoid an over-familiarity with the location of the diamond deposits.

The working of the diamond mines was an organised operation. Usually, a Telugu Brahmin was appointed on a salary to oversee all mining activities. Any diamond that weighed over 10-13 carats would become the property of the king and any person found secreting away stones would be severely punished. Nevertheless, it is quite clear from the accounts of those times that many large diamonds were sold to the French, Portuguese, English and Dutch directly by people who held high posts at the mines.

There was another method by which the mines were allotted to an overseer. Bids were invited and whoever put forward the best offer was given the lease for a fixed period of time. He had to pay not only for this right but was also charged a further amount depending on the number of miners he employed. If none of the bids were successful, the king himself would operate the mines. Most of the diamonds that the king did not keep were officially auctioned.

The diamond merchants, who were from the *bania* community in Gujarat, had settled around Golconda and were so successful in the trading of these precious stones that it came to be monopolised by them and their families for many generations. They sold these stones to other merchants around the country. The principal markets for diamonds were located in Golconda itself, and in Hyderabad.

Needless to say, the Golconda mines were a rich prize that every ruler in the country wished to possess. There are hardly any accurate records about the total output of the mines while they were functioning, but the stones mined at Golconda are probably among the world's biggest and brightest gems. The Mughal rulers at Delhi had long desired to own the region of Golconda. In 1635, Shah Jahan succeeded in making it a peripheral part of the Mughal Empire. By then, war and strife had caused the operations at the mines to suffer, and the quantity of diamonds unearthed was low. By 1653, Shah Jahan appointed his son Aurangzeb the viceroy of the Deccan, who ensured that the mines flourished once again. Aurangzeb was bent on assimilating the complete wealth of Golconda into the Mughal treasury and he nominated Mir Jumla the Commander of the Troops in order to accomplish this mission. Finally, in 1687, during the reign of Aurangzeb, Golconda was seized, and its wealth that had so enchanted conquerors and travellers alike, now became an irrevocable part of the Mughal Empire.

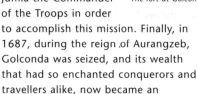

The fort at Golconda.

Man has always been fascinated with the treasures of the earth and has relentlessly sought them. Around the 1950s, the Geological Survey of India conducted a thorough exploration of the diamond mines at Golconda. Guided by experts in the field, they employed new machinery and used contemporary methods, but to no avail. Today, the mines lie completely barren with no hope of any more diamond discoveries. Golconda has become a chapter in history replete with stories of a land where stars, glittering and precious, could once be found on this earth.

THE INDIAN DIAMOND INDUSTRY

Some of the world's most famous diamonds came from India, which has always been centre stage in the dramatic history of these mesmerising gems. The earliest known source of diamonds, India no longer mines them on a large scale. However, it is a forerunner in the gem industry today and a world leader in the manufacture of cut and polished diamonds. Nine out of every ten diamonds used in jewellery worldwide come from India. Today, the diamond mining countries in the world are Russia, Botswana, South Africa, Angola, Namibia, Australia, Zaire, Brazil, Guyana, Venezuela, Guinea, Ivory Coast, Ghana, Tanzania, China, Indonesia and India. The first seven account for over 80 per cent of the world's rough diamond supply.

The Indian diamond industry is mainly involved with cutting, polishing and exporting diamonds. Indian cut and polished diamonds are universally prized, and over the years India has emerged as the largest diamond cutting centre in the world, far exceeding the output of countries such as Israel and Belgium. Although India pioneered in, and was famous for the cutting of small diamonds, today, its craftsmen are equally skilled at cutting all shapes and sizes of stones, and even at faceting coloured diamonds. The main polishing centres of the country are based in Mumbai, Surat, Ahmedabad, Bhavnagar and many small towns in Gujarat. The industry here is so large that it employs one million people, accounting for 95 per cent of the workforce of the world's diamond industry.

The industry as we see it today is a result of perseverance and hard work. For several years after India became independent in 1947, the nation's economy was in the doldrums. As new policies opened several vistas for business and commerce, the diamond industry also began its journey towards progress and development.

Only three decades ago, it was a scattered cottage industry before it gradually evolved into a modern, mechanised, large-scale operation. Today, most of the medium- and large-sized diamond factories are well equipped with state of the art laser machines, bruting lathes and diamond-impregnated scaives.

This structured and rapid growth had an abiding impact on the world jewellery industry. The Indian exports of diamonds increased and in turn augmented the export of designed jewellery. It is well known that Indian jewellery designs have for centuries fascinated everyone, from Indian maharajas to monarchs of faraway lands. In 1999-2000, the gem and jewellery exports accounted for a whopping 22 per cent of India's total merchandise exports.

Indian jewellery was traditionally crafted by family jewellers skilled in a particular style, and was made meticulously by hand. Large exports led to the establishment of factories equipped with the latest modern machinery, and the newest methods in the manufacturing process were employed. India's artisans built on their traditional skills and mastered contemporary techniques to provide the world with jewellery that met international standards. Apart from a host of established houses that design and fashion jewellery, there is a new generation of young designers dominating the world market. Several jewellery design institutes across India are encouraging fresh ideas and talent. The Sardar Patel Centre of Jewellery Design and Manufacture in Surat, based on the Indian Diamond Institute, also in Surat, is one such place. This educational centre is well known for its role in training artisans in the latest techniques. Apart from the Sardar Patel Centre, the Jewellery Product Development Centres in Mumbai, Delhi and Jaipur are also involved in training and promoting young designers through various local and international competitions such as the De Beers Diamond International Awards and the World Gold Council competitions. It is a matter of great pride that several Indian designers have been receiving prizes for the most innovative and breathtakingly beautiful jewellery designs seen in the world today.

The apex body of this dazzling and growing industry is the Gem and Jewellery Export Promotion Council (GJEPC). It has played a major role in consolidating the diverse efforts of several artisans, traders, and exporters, making this dynamic, export-based industry what it is today. The council was set up in 1966 under the auspices of the Ministry of Commerce and has helped forge a better understanding between the diamond industry and the government. Although the chief function of the council is to develop and promote the export of gems and jewellery from India, it also contributes towards establishing a code of ethics and ensuring that fair trade practices are followed. This includes training and looking after the well-being of the craftsmen who work in the industry. In addition, it is a registering authority for all gem exporters and it regulates the industry fairly and cohesively. Its pioneering efforts in forging links between Indian buyers and exporters with their foreign counterparts have led to India holding pride of place in the international diamond arena. Regular seminars, expositions, trade fairs and other promotional activities ensure that the industry remains an evolving force for all its members.

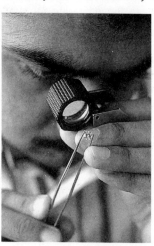

A diamond being minutely examined through a loupe or magnifying glass.

The Indian Diamond Institute in Surat, the Jewellery Product Development Centres in Mumbai, Delhi and Jaipur are all managed by GJEPC. The council also supports related bodies such as the Gem Testing Laboratory based in Jaipur, Rajasthan. Another such body is the Indian Gemmological Institute in Delhi that is at the forefront of training personnel to identify and grade diamonds and other gemstones. Apart from testing gems, this centre also provides training to students at the Gemmological Association and Gem Testing Laboratory of Great Britain.

Having come so far, the Indian diamond industry is again at the threshold of expansion and a new vision. The next step, after establishing itself as a prime manufacturer of cut and polished diamonds, is to excel as a trading centre as well. The GJEPC is continuously developing direct links with countries producing rough diamonds so that these precious stones can travel easily from mines to markets.

The government has also sanctioned the setting up of bonded warehouses, enabling diamonds to be brought into the country to be sold. Diamonds that remain unsold can then be exported without any duty or tax. The government is also constantly liberalising its policies and it has created Export Promotion Zones (EPZ) and Special Economic Zones (SEZ) in order to help and promote the export of gems and jewellery from the country.

With the continual growth of its diamond industry, as well as the unique niche it has carved for itself in the international jewellery arena, India has proved to be successful in ensuring that in spite of its dwindling diamond deposits, it remains an eternally fascinating treasury of the world.

DIAMOND PROCESSING

GRADING

Diamonds are graded according to their colour and clarity, the processes involved being rigidly structured and universally followed by the trade. In the 1930s, the Gemological Institute of America (GIA) was the pioneer in setting up a grading system that is now followed throughout the world. The highest colourless grade is 'D' and each subsequent letter to 'Z' signifies a yellower shade. The nearer a diamond is to the 'D' colour, the rarer and more expensive it will be. The GIA established a scale of eleven grades for clarity from 'F' for flawless to 'I3' for imperfect with different levels in between indicating a diamond's clarity. All historic large diamonds which come up for public auction in the world market are accompanied by a GIA diamond grading report which describes the shape, cut, proportions, finish, clarity, colour, and provides comments along with linear diagrams of the stone.

But what is it that makes a diamond an artefact that is coveted by royals and commoners alike? There are few diamonds less than 20 carats that are important enough to merit special mention unless they have an unusual or unique colour. 'One in a million', is the term given by the diamond trade to collection quality gems. In actual fact though, these diamonds are even rarer than that. The GIA maintains detailed records both of the diamond production of the world and of the stones that it receives for grading. It has estimated the current annual world production of diamonds to be 125 million carats, of which 2 to 2.5 million carats produce faceted, perfectly-coloured pure stones of over a carat, designated D-flawless. In short, only about a fiftieth of all diamonds mined have the size, colour and purity that buyers want. Most of the stones that do not meet these standards are industrials and near-gems, which account for more than 80 per cent of rough diamonds. Large flawless diamonds are among nature's most precious creations.

The GIA reports have estimated that only about 600 such gems a year result in a finished product between one to two carats. In fact, less than 5,000 D-colour diamonds, weighing over half a carat each, are found every year.

CUTTING

There are no records of the first attempts to cut, facet and polish diamonds, however, all evidence points to the fact that these efforts initially took place in India. Lapidaries who crafted stones for Indian emperors had mastered the art of polishing and bruting, that is turning a diamond round and round while holding another diamond against it till the desired shape is achieved. These early precious stones were relatively uncut, probably in keeping with the preference for size rather than brilliance, but over the centuries, skilled craftsmen applied the laws of mathematics to their art, working for hours on a single slender facet till they achieved the perfect diamond shape and cut. Today, these faceted gems are shimmering examples of man's passionate engagement with the earth's most romantic gift.

Diamonds being so hard, it was thought for a long time that they could never be cut. However, Indian artisans had been cutting and polishing other gemstones long before diamonds were discovered. No doubt, the skills they possessed to fashion the softer stones into cabochons and to carve tiny mirror-like facets on the toughest material on earth differed greatly. Indian lapidaries found that a diamond could be ground against another to remove the 'skin', making the stones sparkle. Over the centuries, artisans worked towards a cut that would give the stone maximum brilliance and minimise the loss of weight. Legend has it that by the end of the 17th century, a Venetian named Peruzzi gave the world the full 58-facet brilliant. But it was only in the 20th century that Marcel Tolkowsky worked out the geometry of the modern brilliant cut that we are familiar with today.

People have always been spellbound by the firelike movement within the inert depths of diamonds. This fire, enhanced by skilful faceting, gives the stone its unmatched beauty and lustre. Diamonds are cut into a number of shapes, depending on the nature of the rough stone, the target markets and popular trends. The most sought after shapes are brilliant (round), oval, pear, marquise or navette (boat-shaped),

heart, and emerald (rectangular with cut corners). Other less common shapes are square, table, star, triangular, baguette (slender rectangular), kite and arrow baguette (tapering at one end). The number of facets which reflect light from a stone's tiny sculpted surface vary with each cut, the standard brilliant cut having 58 facets and the star cut, 156 facets.

Cutting a diamond enhances its power to bend light rays (refraction) and break them into all the colours of the rainbow, creating an unsurpassed prismatic brilliance. Today, certain stages are followed in the cutting of a brilliant with 58 facets and these are carried out in most factories all over the world. At first, the rough diamond is examined through a ten-magnification eyeglass called a loupe, and if there is a 'skin' on it, several windows are polished on the surface in order to observe the internal structure. All fissures, bubbles and black spots are polished out. Like timber, diamonds have a grain and its direction is determined in the initial study; they can be later cleaved along the grain or sawn against it.

The rough stone is cut into an octahedron and is sawn into two parts on a wafer-thin disc of phosphor bronze that is impregnated with diamond dust. The disc rotates at a speed of 5,000-10,000 revolutions per minute and a very large stone can take up to two weeks to saw through. The stone is then 'bruted' using one diamond as a tool to shape another. In the earlier days, apprentices learnt to facet diamonds by cutting potatoes with a pocket knife. Today, beginners watch a master cutter, and start their own work with diamonds. The diamond is given a shape that resembles a spinning top with a round flat surface on top and a pointed end below. It is then polished on a flat wheel, like a turntable, that is made of porous iron about an inch thick. The turntable spins 2,500 times a minute and the diamond is held against it in an arm quite similar to a stylus holder on a record player. This process of polishing gradually adds facets with clean sharp edges, which meet each other with absolute precision. A diamond is said to be well cut when

A diamond being polished.

all its facets are clean, sharp, geometrically correct and symmetrical, and when the stone's proportions above and below the girdle match.

The finished gem is often less than half the weight of the original rough stone but it is worth more than twice as much. Although diamonds are cut and polished in twenty-six countries around the world, the important cutting centres are New York, Antwerp, Tel Aviv and Mumbai. The cutters involved in faceting these stones have to be very skilful indeed as it is their talent that unlocks the diamond's fire and brilliance.

CUTS OF DIAMONDS

One of the earliest cuts applied to diamonds was the Mughal cut, which is no longer used today. Sadly, only a few examples of this cut have survived in their original form, chief being the 115.06-carat Taj-i-Mah diamond that is displayed in Tehran. Others such as the Great Mughal and the Great Table diamond, seized by Nadir Shah and taken to Persia in 1739 after his plunder of Delhi, have since been recut.

A Mughal-cut gem had a broad, asymmetrical base, a crown with four shallow facets, or a table, and two or more rows of facets sloping down to the base. This ensured that the original shape of the stone remained unaltered, even though the diamond was covered

with several facets, and often meant that the flaws remained intact.

A fine example of the Mughal cut was the Koh-i-Noor, which was later cut from 186 (old) carats to 105.60 metric carats. There are several critics of this later cutting as the diamond no doubt lost some of its historic character in this endeavour to please the English royalty.

The art of cleaving the diamond along its grain evolved in India. There are references to diamond cutting in the records left by European travellers as far back as the mid-1500s. The 17th-century gem merchant, Jean-Baptiste Tavernier, describes how the grain of the diamond was found: "... each [cutter] has only a steel wheel of about the size of our plates. They place but one stone on each wheel, and pour water incessantly on the wheel until they have found the 'grain' of the stone. ... [Then] they pour on oil. ..."

Mughal-cut diamonds with the rose-cut in 'parab' (straight flat) or 'mukhalasi' (faceted flat) shape were seen in India till 1947, but the fire and brilliance created by the modern cuts captured the fancy of the Indian market and the older cuts went out of fashion.

Although diamonds were being used in jewellery made for Indian royalty for many centuries, the Western world realised the true potential of this sparkling gem only in the 17th century. This was the time when Jean-Baptiste Tavernier travelled between Europe and the Golconda mines in India, and carried away with him some of the most exquisite diamonds ever discovered. It was also during this time that diamond cutting became more advanced.

Prior to this period, three cuts were used quite prominently:

Table cut: The table cut gave the diamond a large flat facet on top.

Rose cut: Simulating a rosebud, this cut gave the diamond a flat base and tiny triangular facets leading up to a point on the top. The small, polished surfaces trapped light within the stone and enhanced its brilliance.

Early brilliant cut: This cut added more facets to the bottom of a diamond, making it more lustrous.

Around 1929, when Art Deco jewellery was in fashion, several cuts, some new and others not so new, were employed. Chief amongst them were the following:

Brilliant cut: A basic circular cut that consisted of 16 facets was earlier used on smaller diamonds. Since this cut did not do much to enhance the gem's brilliance, a need for improvement was felt by jewellers the world over. The earliest version of the modern brilliant (round) cut was an old European cut which had a small table and a large crown. Another of its ancestors was the Mazarin cut, named after Cardinal Jules Mazarin, an avid French diamond collector who oversaw its creation in 1615. This cut had 16 facets above the cushion-shaped girdle and 16 below it. Due to this symmetry in the number of facets above and below, this cut was also referred to as the double cut.

The circular cut with 58 facets, purportedly crafted by the Venetian lapidary Peruzzi, was known as the brilliant cut. It created more sparkle than the previous cuts and was popular till 1914, when Marcel Tolkowsky, a young engineer, drew the modern brilliant, also with 58 facets, but with a mathematical precision. The success of this cut lay in its ability to capture light through the top facet and hold it within to create fire and brilliance.

Step cut: Here, all facets are four sided and in steps, or rows, both above and below the girdle. All facets are parallel to the girdle and therefore, except for those at the corners, they are long and usually narrow. The number of rows or steps may vary, although the usual number is three on the crown and three on the pavilion.

Marquise cut: This boat-shaped cut with points at either end, was designed in France in the 1740s. It got its name

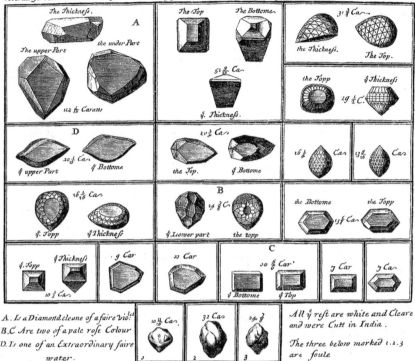

Tavernier's drawings of the diamonds sold to King Louis XIV of France.

from the Marquise de Pompadour, the mistress of King Louis XV. This cut, in combination with the emerald and square cut, is also called a fancy cut.

Emerald cut: The emerald cut was used principally for emeralds but became popular with diamonds because of its clean lines. A square or rectangular cut with several facets on the crown and pavilion, and with chamfered or diagonally-cut corners, it is usually employed in long, rough diamonds.

Square cut: This cut is characterised by a square table and four step-cut facets.

Baguette cut: The baguette cut, which derived its name from the eponymous French bread, has a long, slim shape with sharp, clean lines. Initially, the long, rectangular shape had rounded corners, but it later developed into a clean geometric rectangle.

Princess cut: This cut is a combination of the brilliant and step cut. Depending on its basic shape, the diamond is either cut as a square or truncated carré. If the surface of the octahedron is well maintained, a square cut forms with sharp edges. But if the corners of the stone are slightly damaged, then they are truncated.

QUOTES AND REFERENCES

Ever since man has known diamonds, he has been obsessed by them, conjuring up fascinating stories about their origin and assigning special powers to them. As the source of these precious stones, India attracted many jewellers and scholars who left records of their visits to the diamond mines and to the courts of the great Mughals.

GARUDA-PURĀNAM

Garuda-Purānam, probably written before the 10th century AD, is one of the eighteen great Purānas, containing accounts on religious and secular subjects such as ceremonies and rituals, astronomy, astrology and gemmology. The following excerpt is a discourse on diamonds.

There lived in ancient time a demon, named Vala. Vala conquered the god Indra and his celestials, and reigned supreme and invincible in the universe. The gods, on the occasion of a religious sacrifice, jocularly asked him to play the part of the animal of the sacrifice. This Vala consented to do and pledged his word for the performance of the part and suffered himself to be bound at the sacrificial stake. Whereupon the gods turned the jest into earnest and killed the invincible Vala in that mockery of a religious sacrifice. Thus Vala yielded up his ghost for the good of the universe and the welfare of the gods, and, behold, the severed limbs and members of his sanctified body, were converted into the seeds of gems.

Then the gods and the Yakshas and the Siddhas and the Nagas eagerly rushed to collect those seeds of gems. ... some of which dropped down on earth, through the violent concussion of the air. Wherever they dropped, whether in oceans, rivers, mountains or wildernesses there origined mines of those gems through the celestial potency of their respective seeds. ...

The least particle of bone of the conquerer of Indra, falling or dropping down from the sky in a country, germinates diamond-crystals of varied shapes. The eight regions or divisions of the country in which diamond is found, are the Himalayas, the Matangas, the provinces of Anga, Saurastra, Poundra, Kalinga, Koshala, the basin of the river Venva, and the country of the Souveras. Diamonds found in the region of the Himalayas, are tinged with a little copper-colour, while those found in the basin of the Venva are coloured like the disc of the full moon. Diamonds found in the country of the Souvera, are possessed of a lustre similar to the deep shade of a black rain cloud, while those found in the country of Sourashtra, shine with a copper-coloured effulgence. Diamonds found in the country of Kalinga, are coloured like the molten gold, while those found in Koshala are yellow. Diamonds found in the country of Poundra, are coloured blue, while those found in the regions of the Matangas, are yellowish in their hue.

Gods are supposed to dwell in a particle of diamond, wherever found, which is possessed of a clear, light shade and the usual commendable features, is smooth and even at the sides, and is divested of all threatening traits such as scratches, dot like impressions, marks of crow's feet, or clouding impurities in its interior. Coloured diamonds, should be regarded as presided over by different divinities according to their respective hues. Green, white, yellow, brown, blue and copper-coloured diamonds are ascribed to the direct tutelage of the Sun, Varuna, Indra, the Fire-God, the Lord of the Pitris and the Maruts, respectively.

A Brahmana is enjoined to wear a diamond which is coloured like a conch shell, or a Kumuda flower or a white crystal, whereas a Kshatriya should wear one that is coloured brownish yellow like the eyes of a hare. A diamond possessed of a soft greenish colour like the tender leaves of a plantain tree, prove beneficial to a man of the Vaishya class, while a Shudra would do well to wear a diamond that has a lustre like that of a newly washed sword. Diamonds which are coloured yellow or possessed of a hue like that of a coral or a Java flower, (China Rose) should be held as fit only for the use of a king and would prove positively harmful to any man occupying a lower position in life. A king in his capacity of the lord of all the castes, is privileged to wear diamonds of any colour he pleases, provided they are not vitiated by the prohibited features, whereas such a conduct on the part of an ordinary man, is sure to be attended with evil consequences.

A diamond possessed of a double or dubious shade or colour, should be looked upon as portending dire calamities like the birth of an illegitimate or half caste child in the family, etc. A diamond should not be used only with a look to the caste or class it specifically belongs to, inasmuch as a diamond possessed of all the commendable features proves as a source of boundless prosperity to its wearer, whereas a diamond vitiated by any of the condemnable traits, turns out to be a spring of unmitigated evil.

A diamond with one of its angles or horns broken or mutilated, or looking as if scratched, withered or trampled down, should not be retained in the household, though otherwise possessed of all commendable features, as it would certainly bring hosts of unsuspected evils in its train. The goddess of wealth is sure to part company with a person who is impudent enough to wear a diamond which emits a red glare through one of its mutilated horns or angles and looks cloudy and impure at the centre. A diamond scratched … and which appears to be painted with stripes of red in the inside, robs the decent competence of its wearer, and subsequently brings on his death and ruin. A diamond found in its natural state in … a mine, is either hexagonal or octagonal in shape or appears like a polygon of twelve sides with all its exterior angles or points prominently marked and equally sharpened.

A diamond, cut into the shape of a regular hexagon with well-smoothed sides and well-marked points or angles, and shedding a clear prismatic lustre from the inside and divested of all the harmful traits described in the books on gems and precious stones, is to be rarely found even amidst the treasures of crowned heads. Prosperity, long life, increase of wives and progeny and domestic animals, and the bringing home of a teeming harvest, attend on the use of a diamond, keen and well marked in its points, clear in lustre and divested of the characteristic baneful traits. Serpents, tigers, and thieves fly from the presence of a person wearing such a diamond. Fatal and dreadful poisons, secretly administered, prove inoperative in his system and all his possessions enjoy a sort of immunity from acts of incendiarism or erosions by water. ...

A diamond, devoid of all the characteristic blemishes and weighing twenty tandulam in weight, and worn by a man, should be regarded as double in value of the standard of appraising used in respect of ascertaining the water, lustre price and the commendable traits of diamond. Fractions such as $\frac{1}{3}$, $\frac{1}{6}$, $\frac{1}{10}$, $\frac{1}{15}$, $\frac{1}{80}$ or $\frac{1}{100}$ should respectively [be] used in computing the price of a diamond, wherever it would be found necessary to appraise a diamond by the standard of another diamond of greater weight and brilliancy. An infinitesimally small fraction in such an instance, should be computed as equal to a thousandth part of the latter in price. Eight seeds of white sesamum equal a Tandulam in weight, and the use of a diamond weighing less than even the latter standard-measure, is not prohibited. A diamond possessed of all the commendable traits and found to float on the water in test, should be worn by a man in exclusion of all the other gems happening to be in his possession.

A diamond found to be affected with small defects whether visible or invisible to the naked eyes, should be appraised at a price equal to a tenth part of that of a diamond of similar water and weight, but devoid of all such blemishes. A diamond marked with many a patent defect, whether great, or small should not be appraised at a price even equal to a hundredth part of that of a similar stainless diamond. A diamond otherwise defective, but set in a prepared article of ornament, should be valued at a very low price. A diamond of the first water, but found to be otherwise possessed of any of the condemnable traits, should not be set in a royal ornament even for the purpose of decoration. Diamonds are prohibited as articles of female wear, as they are possessed of the mystic virtues of making them sterile and unhappy. A diamond which has a stunted, elongated or a flattened look like that of a thrashed paddy, should be looked upon as devoid of all commendable features.

Imitation diamonds are made by skilful artisans with such substances as the iron, the Pushparaga (topaz) the Gomeda, the Vaiduryyam (lapis-lazuli), the crystal and the glass, and hence their genuineness should be made to be tested by experts, well-versed in the art of recognising and appraising precious stones. A diamond offered for sale, should be put to such tests, as scratching, shana (emery wheel) and immersion in alkaline solutions. A diamond would scratch all other metals or gems, such as the iron, etc., without being scratched by any of them in return. *(pp. 180-186)*

MEMOIRS OF ZEHĪR-ED-DĪN MUHAMMED BĀBUR

The Mughal dynasty was founded in India in 1526 by a Timurid prince, Babur. Almost all Mughal emperors had their biographies written as a testimony to the riches of their court and their imperial conquests. The memoirs of Babur, written in the 16th century, were the first of these priceless documents. Here Babur describes how he received the Koh-i-noor from his son, Humayun.

On Friday, the 22nd of Rajeb, I halted in the suburbs of Agra, at the palace of Suleimān Fermūli. As this position was very far from the fort, I next morning moved and took up my quarters at the palace of Jalāl Khān Jighat. The people of the fort had put off Humāiūn, who arrived before me, with excuses; and he, on his part, considering that they were under no control, and wishing to prevent their plundering the treasure, had taken a position to shut up the issues from the place.

Bikermajīt, a Hindu, who was Raja of Gwāliār, had governed that country for upwards of a hundred years. Sikander had remained several years in Agra, employed in an attempt to take Gwāliār. Afterwards, in the reign of Ibrahīm, Azīm Humāiūn Sarwāni invested it for some time, made several attacks, and at length succeeded in gaining it by treaty, Shamsābād being given as an indemnification. In the battle in which Ibrahīm was defeated, Bikermajīt was sent to hell. Bikermajīt's family, and the heads of his clan, were at this moment in Agra. When Humāiūn arrived, Bikermajīt's people attempted to escape, but were taken by the parties which Humāiūn had placed upon the watch, and put in custody. Humāiūn did not permit them to be plundered. Of their own free will they presented to Humāiūn a *peshkesh*, consisting of a quantity of jewels and precious stones. Among these was one famous diamond, which had been acquired by Sultan Alā ed dīn. It is so valuable, that a judge of diamonds valued it at half of the daily expense of the whole world. It is about eight *mishkals*. On my arrival, Humāiūn presented it to me as a *peshkesh*, and I gave it back to him as a present. *(pp. 191-192)*

THE AKBAR NĀMĀ by Abu-l-Fazl

In the biographies of the Mughal emperors can be found innumerable references to the exchange of precious gifts. In the following account from the Akbar Nāmā, written in the late 16th century, it is revealed how Humayun acquired the Koh-i-noor.

Everyone, small and great, in Hindūstān experienced the royal kindness and balminess. Out of his ... kindness, the mother, children and dependants of Sultān Ibrāhīm were made partakers of his bounty and special stipends were assigned to them. An allowance of a property worth seven *lakhs* of *tankas* was made to Ibrāhīm's mother. Similarly pensions were bestowed on his other relatives. The distracted world was soothed. His Majesty Jahānbānī Jannat-āshīyānī who had previously arrived at Agra, presented a diamond eight *misqāls* in weight and which was valued by jewellers at one-half of the daily expenditure of the inhabited world. They said that this diamond had belonged to the treasury of Sultān 'Alā'u-d-dīn (Khiljī). He (Humāyūn) got it from the family of Bikramājīt, the Rāja of Gwālīār. His Majesty, from the nobility of his nature, first accepted it and then returned it to him (Humāyūn) as a present. ...

His Majesty Jahānbānī on the day of the great festival presented to the Shāh as the gift of a traveller a diamond of great value—worth the revenues of countries and climes, together with 250 Badakhshān rubies. Without a doubt, all the expenditure which the Shāh, whether from his privy purse, or through his officers, incurred on account of his Majesty Jahānbānī from the time of his entering the country to his exit therefrom was hereby repaid more than four times over. *(pp. 247-248, 439)*

TRAVELS IN THE MOGUL EMPIRE by François Bernier

In the 17th century, Mughal India had a sumptuous court that attracted travellers and ambassadors from every country. François Bernier, a French intellectual and secretary to a famous scholar, Pierre Gassendi, arrived in India in 1658. He was employed as a doctor to the Mughal emperor Aurangzeb. Here Bernier describes the Peacock Throne.

The King appeared seated upon his throne, at the end of the great hall, in the most magnificent attire. His vest was of white and delicately flowered satin, with a silk and gold embroidery of the finest texture. The turban, of gold cloth, had an aigrette whose base was composed of diamonds of an extraordinary size and value, besides an Oriental topaz, which may be pronounced unparalleled, exhibiting a lustre like the sun. A necklace of immense pearls, suspended from his neck, reached to the stomach, in the same manner as many of the *Gentiles*

wear their strings of beads. The throne was supported by six massy feet, said to be of solid gold, sprinkled over with rubies, emeralds, and diamonds. I cannot tell you with accuracy the number or value of this vast collection of precious stones, because no person may approach sufficiently near to reckon them, or judge of their water and clearness; but I can assure you that there is a confusion of diamonds, as well as other jewels, and that the throne, to the best of my recollection, is valued at four *Kourours* of *Roupies*. I observed elsewhere that a *Lecque* is one hundred thousand *roupies*, and that a *Kourour* is a hundred *Lecques*; so that the throne is estimated at forty millions of *roupies*, worth sixty millions of pounds [livres] or thereabouts. It was constructed by *Chah-Jehan*, the father of *Aureng-Zebe*, for the purpose of displaying the immense quantity of precious stones accumulated successively in the treasury from the spoils of ancient Rajas and *Palans*, and the annual presents to the Monarch, which every *Omrah* is bound to make on certain festivals. The construction and workmanship of the throne are not worthy of the materials; but two peacocks, covered with jewels and pearls, are well conceived and executed.

They were made by a workman of astonishing powers, a *Frenchman* by birth … who, after defrauding several of the Princes of *Europe*, by means of false gems, which he fabricated with peculiar skill, sought refuge in the *Great Mogol's* court, where he made his fortune. *(pp. 268-269)*

TRAVELS IN INDIA by Jean-Baptiste Tavernier

**VOYAGES
DES INDES**

LIVRE SECOND.

DESCRIPTION HISTORIQUE
& politique de l'Empire du Grand Mogol.

CHAPITRE PREMIER.

Jean-Baptiste Tavernier, a French jeweller and gem merchant, made six trips to India between the years 1631 to 1668. He was fascinated by the numerous jewels and precious stones owned by the Mughal emperors. During his journeys to India, he would purchase large pearls and gemstones which he would then sell, primarily to the members of the European royalty. Tavernier was invited by the great Mughal emperor Aurangzeb to his court and was asked by him to see his jewels, which are described here.

On the first day of November 1665 I went to the palace to take leave of the Emperor, but he said that he did not wish me to depart without having

seen his jewels, and witnessing the splendour of his fête.

Early in the morning of the next day five or six of the Emperor's officers and others on behalf of Nawāb Ja'far Khān, announced that the Emperor wished to see me. Immediately on my arrival at the Court the two custodians of the royal jewels … accompanied me into the presence of His Majesty; and after I had made him the customary salutation, they conducted me into a small apartment, which is at one of the ends of the hall where the Emperor was seated on his throne, and whence he was able to see us. I found in this apartment 'Ākil Khān, chief of the jewel treasury, who, when he saw us, commanded four of the imperial eunuchs to bring the jewels, which were carried in two large wooden trays lacquered with gold leaf, and covered with small cloths made expressly for the purpose. … After these trays were uncovered, and all the pieces had been counted three times over, a list was prepared by three scribes who were present. For the Indians do everything with great circumspection and patience, and when they see any one who acts with precipitation, or becomes angry, they gaze at him without saying anything, and smile as if he were a madman.

The first piece which 'Ākil Khān placed in my hands was the great diamond, which is a round rose, very high at one side. At the basal margin it has a small notch and flaw inside. Its water is beautiful, and it weighs $319\frac{1}{2}$ ratis, which are equal to 280 of our carats—the rati being $\frac{7}{8}$th of our carat. When Mīr Jumla, who betrayed the King of Golkonda, his master, presented this stone to Shāhjahān, to whose side he attached himself, it was then in the rough, and weighed 900 ratis, which are equivalent to $787\frac{1}{2}$ carats; and it had several flaws. ...

After I had fully examined this splendid stone, and returned it into the hands of 'Ākil Khān, he showed me another stone, pear-shaped, of good form and fine water, and also three other table diamonds, two clear, and the other with some little black spots. Each weighed 55 to 60 ratis, and the pear $62\frac{1}{2}$. Subsequently he showed me a jewel set with twelve diamonds, each stone of 15 to 16 ratis, and all roses. In the middle a heart-shaped rose of good water, but with three small flaws, and this rose weighed about 35 or 40 ratis. Also a jewel set with seventeen diamonds, half of them table and half rose, the largest of which could not weigh more than 7 or 8 ratis, with the exception of the one in the middle, which weighed about 16. All these stones are of first-class water, clean and of good form, and the most beautiful ever found. Also two grand pear-shaped pearls, one weighing about 70 ratis. ... Also a pearl button, which

might weigh from 55 to 60 ratis. ... Also a round pearl of great perfection, a little flat on one side, which weighs 56 ratis. ... Also three other round pearls, each of 25 to 28 ratis. ... Also a perfectly round pearl of $36\frac{1}{2}$ ratis, of a lively white, and perfect in every respect. It is the only jewel which Aurangzeb, who reigns at present, has himself purchased on account of its beauty, for the rest either came to him from Dārā Shikoh, his eldest brother, he having appropriated them after he had caused his head to be cut off, or they were presents made to him after he ascended the throne. ...

'Ākil Khān also placed in my hands, for he allowed me to examine all at my ease, two other pearls, perfectly round and equal, each of which weighed $25\frac{1}{4}$ ratis. ... Also two chains, one of pearls and rubies of different shapes pierced like the pearls; the other of pearls and emeralds, round and bored. ... In the middle of the chain of rubies there is a large emerald of the 'old rock', cut into a rectangle, and of high colour, but with many flaws. It weighs about 30 ratis. In the middle of the chain of emeralds there is an oriental amethyst, a long table, weighing about 40 ratis, and the perfection of beauty. Also a balass ruby cut en cabochon, of fine colour and clean pierced at the apex, and weighing 17 melscals. Six melscals make one once (French). Also another cabochon ruby of perfect colour, but slightly flawed and pierced at the apex, which weighs 12 melscals. Also an oriental topaz of very high colour cut in eight panels, which 6 melscals, but on one side it has a small white fog within.

These, then, are the jewels of the

Great Mogul, which he ordered to be shown to me as a special favour which he has never manifested to any other Frank; and I have held them all in my hand, and examined them with sufficient attention and leisure to be enabled to assure the reader that the description which I have just given is very exact. ... *(Vol I, pp. 314-319)*

Tavernier describes how diamonds were polished at the Ramallakota Mine.

If the stone is clean they ... do not venture to give it any form, for fear of reducing the weight. But if it has a small flaw, or any spots, or small black or red grit, they cover the whole of the stone with facettes in order that its defects may not be seen, and if it has a very small flaw they conceal it by the edge of one of the facettes. But it should be remarked that the merchant prefers a black point in a stone to a red one. When there is a red one the stone is roasted, and the point becomes black. I learned this trick at length so well that when I examined a parcel of stones which came from this mine, and saw that there were facettes on any of them, especially small facettes, I was certain that there was some speck or flaw in the stone.

There are at this mine numerous diamond-cutters, and each has only a steel wheel of about the size of our plates. They place but one stone on each wheel, and pour water incessantly on the wheel until they have found the 'grain' of the stone. The 'grain' being found, they pour on oil and do not spare diamond dust, although it is expensive, in order to make the stone run faster, and they weight it much more heavily than we do. ...

The Indians are unable to give the stones such a lively polish as we give them in Europe; this, I believe, is due to the fact that their wheels do not run so smoothly as ours. For, being made of steel, in order to grind it on the emery, of which it has need every twenty-four hours, it has to be taken off the tree, and it cannot be replaced so as to run as evenly as it should do. If they possessed the iron wheel like ours, for which not emery but the file is required, it is not necessary to remove it from the tree in order to file it, and they could give the stones a better polish than they do. I have stated that it is necessary to rub the wheel with emery or to file it every twenty-four hours, and it is desirable that this should be done every twelve hours if the workman is not lazy. For when the stone has run a certain time, the part of the wheel where it has pressed becomes polished like a mirror, and if the place be not roughened by emery or the file, the powder does not stick to it. When it does adhere more work can be done in one hour than in two when there is none on the wheel.

Although a particular diamond may be by nature hard, having, so to speak, a kind of knot, such as is seen in wood, the Indian diamond-cutters would not hesitate to cut such a stone, although our diamond-cutters in Europe would experience great difficulty in doing so, and as a general rule would be unwilling to undertake it; but the Indians are paid something extra for their trouble. *(Vol II, pp. 44-46)*

GLOSSARY

baguette: a gem that is cut in a long, rectangular shape

banias: a community of merchants

brilliant: a diamond cut in a round shape with 58 facets

bruting: the process by which a diamond is made round in shape

cabochon: a gem polished but not faceted

carat: the unit of weight used for measuring all gems including diamonds. One metric carat = 0.2053 grams. Unless specified otherwise, 'carat' in this book means metric carat

carré: a square step-cut gem

cleavage: the splitting of a gem along a plane, due to a fault in its crystalline structure

crown: the top half of a faceted gem, which lies above the girdle

culet: the pointed underside tip of a diamond, sometimes polished till slightly flattened

cushion shape: a gem with such a shape has a rectangular or square girdle with rounded corners, as well as sides that are frequently rounded

emerald cut: a square or rectangular shaped-cut

facet: a flat, polished surface of a gem

fancy: a diamond of uncommon natural colour, valued because of its rarity

fire: the internal sparkle created within a

diamond by cutting and polishing

flaw: a speck, crack, or fissure in a gem

girdle: the outer circumference between the crown and pavilion of a faceted gem. It is the widest part of the stone

grain: the texture or arrangement of constituent particles in a gem, which determine the procedure for cutting

mangelin: an old Indian weight for gems equal to roughly 1.40 metric carats

marquise: a polished boat-shaped gem with points at both ends

Mughal cut: an old style of cutting in which the shape of the gem remained largely unaltered

pavé: a setting where gems are placed very close together to cover a surface

pavilion: the lower half of a faceted gem, which lies below the girdle

rose cut: an old style of cutting; the base is one large flat facet topped with numerous facets that give the crown a dome shape

rough: irregularly shaped, uncut diamonds found in nature

table: large flat surface on the top of a gem

table cut: an old style of cutting where the diamond was given a large flat facet on the top, with more than four corners

water: the transparency of a diamond

SELECT BIBLIOGRAPHY

ABU-L-FAZL. The Akbar Nama. Vol. I. Translated by H Beveridge. Reprinted from Bibliotheca Indica. Delhi: Rare Books, 1972

BABUR. Memoirs of Zehir-ed-Din Muhammed Babur. 2 vols. Translated by John Leyden and William Erskine. Oxford: Oxford University Press, 1921

BALFOUR, IAN. Famous Diamonds. London: Christie's, Manson and Woods Ltd, 1997

BERNIER, FRANÇOIS. Travels in the Mogul Empire, AD 1656-1668. Edited by Archibald Constable. Revised edition. Westminster:

Archibald Constable and Company, 1891

GARUDA-PURANAM, of the Chowkhamba Sanskrit Studies, Vol. LXVII. Translated by Manmatha Nath Dutt Shastri. 2d ed. Varanasi: The Chowkhamba Sanskrit Series Office, 1968

GREGORIETTI, GUIDO. Jewellery Through the Ages. London: Hamlyn, 1970

KHALIDI, OMAR. Romance of the Golconda Diamonds. Ahmedabad: Mapin Publishing Pvt Ltd, 1999

MORROW, ANN. Highness. London: Grafton, 1986

PRIOR, KATHERINE, AND JOHN ADAMSON. *Maharajas' Jewels.* Paris: Éditions Assouline, 2000

ROBINSON, ANDREW. *Maharaja: The Spectacular Heritage of Princely India.* London: Thames and Hudson, 1988

SCARISBRICK, DIANA. *Ancestral Jewels.* London: Andre Deutsch Ltd, 1989

SEN, N B. *Glorious History of the Koh-i-Noor Diamond.* New Delhi: New Book Society of

India, 1970

STREETER, EDWIN. *The Great Diamonds of the World.* London: George Bell & Sons, 1882

TAVERNIER, JEAN-BAPTISTE. *Travels in India.* Vols. I and II. Translated by V Ball. 2d ed. London: Oxford University Press, 1925

TWINING, LORD. *A History of the Crown Jewels of Europe.* London: B.T. Batsford Ltd, 1960

UNTRACHT, OPPI. *Traditional Jewelry of India.* London: Thames and Hudson, 1997

ILLUSTRATIONS *A listing of archival material*

attire. Artist unknown

101 H H Ranjitsinghji, Jam Saheb of Nawanagar. Photogravure. Photographer unknown. *Forty Years of the Rajkumar College*. 1911

102 Mir Osman Ali Khan, Nizam VII. Photograph by Deen Dayal. 1911

106 Jacques Arpels and Maharaja of Baroda. Photographer unknown. 1947

107 Sita Devi, Maharani of Baroda, and her son Sayaji Rao Prataprao Gaekwad. Photographer unknown. *c* 1949

108 *View of the palace of Agra, from the river.* Engraving by an unknown artist. *c* 1850

112 (**top**) The Nizam diamond. Drawing by Henry Piddington. Reproduced in R M Shipley, *Famous Diamonds of the World;* (**bottom left**) Afzal Mahal, Chow Mahalla Palace. Photographer unknown; (**bottom right**) Mahboob Ali Pasha, sixth Nizam of Hyderabad. Photograph by Deen Dayal. *c* 1890

116 Same as page 102

118 (**bottom**) *H. H. Maharaja Sir Jagatjit Singh Bahadur, G.C.S.I. of Kapurthala State* (1872-1949). Postcard

119 Cotton market, Bombay. Photograph by William Johnson. 1858

121 Ramallakota Mine, Golconda. Sketch by an unknown artist

129 Diamonds sold to King Louis XIV of France. Drawing by Jean-Baptiste Tavernier. *Les Six Voyages de Jean Baptiste Tavernier*. 1676

135 Title page of an early edition of *Voyages des Indes* (*Travels in India*). 1681

CREDITS

Bridgeman Art Library 29, 30, 49, 62-63, 67, 70-71, 80, 93, 97, (Peter Willi) 33, (Stair Sainty Matthiesen Gallery, New York) 44-45, (Bonhams, London) 50, (Smithsonian Institution, Washington DC) 48, 52-53, 113 *top left*

Courtesy of the Trustees of the **Chhatrapati Shivaji Maharaj Vastu Sangrahalaya** (formerly the Prince of Wales Museum of Western India) 77

© **Christie's Images Ltd** 3, 11 *centre*, 27, 69, 72, 73, 75, 87, 96, 99, 103 *centre* & *right*, 104, 105, 109, 113 *bottom, centre right*, 118 *top*

De Beers 9, 55 *top*, 59, 66, 76, 106 *top*, 113 *top centre; bottom left; bottom, centre left;* & *bottom right*

Dinodia Photo Library (Hari Mahidhar) 41, 127, (Jehangir Sorabjee) 55 *bottom*, (Mahendra Patil) 56, (Pramod Mistry) 114, (Nitin Kelvalkar) 122, (Vinay Parelkar) 124

Government of India, Ministry of Tourism and Culture, Department of Culture 6-7, 115

Crown copyright; **Historic Royal Palaces** 11 *right*, 12 *top*, 18, 22

Courtesy **Monisha Bharadwaj** 58, 65, 70, 78, 79 *top*, 81, 83, 88, 92, 100, 102, 112 *bottom right*, 116

Courtesy of the Department of Museums, **Museum & Picture Gallery, Baroda** 25

Courtesy **Omar Khalidi**. *Romance of the Golconda Diamonds* 20, 121

Phillips Antiques 2, 4, 12 *bottom*, 13, 16, 17, 19, 23, 34, 35 *bottom*, 47, 57, 71, 74, 84-85, 85, 89, 90 *bottom*, 91, 101, 108, 112 *bottom left*, 118 *bottom*, 119

Private Collection 21

Photo © **RMN** 40, 43, (Thierry Ollivier) 14-15, (Louvre) 11 *left*, 35 *top*, (Martine Beck Coppola/Louvre) 37, (G Blot) 38, (J Schormans) 39, (Louvre) 42

Royal Ontario Museum, © ROM 10, 60, 61, 64

Russian Diamond Fund 5, 28, 31, 79 *bottom*

Courtesy **San Diego Museum of Art** 82

Sotheby's 90 *top*, 94, 95

Staatlichen Kunstsammlungen, Dresden cover, 110, 111

Van Cleef and Arpels 106 *bottom*, 107

Victoria and Albert Museum 86

INDEX

Page numbers in bold refer to illustrations only

ACKNOWLEDGEMENTS

I owe thanks to scores of people around the world for their help with this book. It would not have been possible without the prompt and enthusiastic support of De Beers, London and Mumbai; Christie's, London, Geneva and Mumbai; Sotheby's, London; Garrard; Van Cleef and Arpels, Paris; Cartier, London; and Harry Winston Inc, New York. My personal thanks to my mother Vimla Patil for her encouragement, and to my publisher Padmini Mirchandani for her faith in me. A tip of the hat to Meera Ahuja at India Book House for her perseverance and humour through thick and thin, and to Monisha Ahmed and Shikha Gupta for their many hours of scrutinising and editing the manuscript.

ISBN 81-7508-326-3

TEXT
© 2002 Monisha Bharadwaj

SERIES DESIGN
PMDL Design Private Limited

GENERAL EDITOR
Monisha Ahmed

PUBLISHED BY
India Book House Pvt Ltd
412 Tulsiani Chambers
Nariman Point, Mumbai 400 021, India
Tel 91 22 284 0165   Fax 91 22 283 5099
E-mail ibhpub@vsnl.com